For Pam,
— with much love,

Delhi, 19 January 1987

THE NEW INDIAN CINEMA

The New Indian Cinema

ARUNA VASUDEV

First published 1986
MACMILLAN INDIA LIMITED
Delhi Bombay Calcutta Madras
Associated companies throughout the world

SBN 33390 928 3

Published by S G Wasani for Macmillan India Limited, 2/10 Ansari Road.
Daryaganj, New Delhi 110 002 :
Printed at Konark Press, Delhi-92

PREFACE

To watch a movement take birth and take shape, to be 'in the thick of it, sharing the experience', maintaining a distance is not easy. Objectivity gets stretched when one has seen the struggle from the inside, understood the strain, recognised the intention. Tolerance becomes a danger, obscuring one's own position and preference.

In 1962-63 I was at the Institut des Hautes Etudes Cinematographiques, the film school in Paris, when I heard that a film institute had been set up at Pune. In 1966, when I was back in Delhi and made my first short film, my cameraman A.K. Goorha was one of the earliest graduates from the Pune Institute. In the years that followed, as I moved from filmmaking to writing about cinema, many of the directors were friends, whose early attempts and later triumphs were something all of us who cared about cinema shared in. There was also a sense of pride in the genesis of another language of film in India. Just as now, twenty years later, there is a sense of anxiety about the appropriation of that language and the direction in which the movement seems to be headed. Within its heart a split is becoming increasingly apparent, a split between filmmakers who prefer to express ideas in ways that average audiences would be able to grasp and those who, with Jean Genet, are interested 'not so much in ideas as in the shape of ideas'. As audiences and the urban intelligentsia confuse content with form, labelling as 'art' anything that has a 'serious' subject, those for whom cinema is more an art than an instrument of social change, are being marginalised as incomprehensible to the ordinary viewer and therefore irrelevant.

The debate then moves on to other ground than the familiar one of art versus commerce. It is the dilemma of the 'new' filmmaker. It is shared by the artist, the writer, the poet, the painter. Their conflicts are born out of the imperative of the times they live in. In a developing society, is it more important to reach audiences with ideas that make a direct connection with their lives through characters they can identify with, or to explore the medium in ways that quicken the imagination?

There are as many subjects for debate as there are themes for filming and ways in which they can be filmed. But that is not the point here. The aim of this book is to provide an introductory overview of the evolution of an alternate cinema in India and the attitudes that grew with it and around it. The first chapter is in the nature of an overture to this movement; the conditions that gave rise to it and the points from which it took flight. The second and third chapters provide a context, tracing the work of its immediate predecessors, those who gave it its impetus and direction and remain a part of it.

From its inception, from the moment the opportunities arose, the new cinema took on so many shapes, in so many languages, that giving the book a structure posed enormous problems. A chronological narration was out of the question; it left no room for cross currents. Classifying the directors according to region and language was not the best solution because many of them work in more than one language, and 'regionalism' is something one would prefer to avoid. However certain characteristics other than language unite the contemporary Bengali filmmakers, as certain themes are common to those from Karnataka. Adoor Gopalakrishnan and Aravindan happen to be from Kerala and use the same spoken language but their film language is totally dissimilar. On the other hand, there are directors who use Marathi as the language but their sensibility is akin to those working in Hindi. A kind of 'middle' cinema placing its stress on a realist aesthetic crosses all frontiers of region and language.

Chapter 9, intended to be confined exclusively to those filmmakers for whom the shape of the film is as significant as its substance, and who work from a deep understanding of the nature and potential of the medium, proved to be an impossibility. It was, for instance, difficult to abstract Adoor Gopalakrishnan and Aravindan from their links with the situation in Kerala, and place them in this chapter where they rightfully belong.

Ultimately one surrenders, realising that this is a stream of highly individualistic personalities who refuse to fall into any pattern. And so, one is obliged to impose some kind of shape, arbitrarily, so that those reading the book are not totally at sea.

The temptation to linger and analyse had to be resisted as a *tour d'horizon* of this nature is not the place for critical essays on a selected number of directors. To give such a perspective without legitimising all work is not easy. My own position and preference for a cinema that breaks national boundaries to speak the universal language of those for whom cinema is above all an art, I hope, emerges out of the manner of the writing.

I am grateful to many colleagues and friends for their assistance. P.K. Nair, Shampa Banerjee, Chidananda Das Gupta, B.D. Garga, generously parted with photographs, the Directorate of Film Festivals, the National Film Development Corporation and the Ministry of Information and Broadcasting arranged film screenings and provided information and photographs without all of which it would have been impossible to complete the book.

Discussion, argument, exchange, serve to crystallise concepts and interpretations, particularly when one is in the midst of events as they are taking place. One does not have the advantage of a perspective that distance in time and place can offer. But friends in the right time and place are invaluable. I drew on Inder Malhotra's deep inside knowledge of recent political happenings, with Ashis Nandy, Nissim Ezekiel, Chidananda Das Gupta, Ashish Rajadhyaksha challenging ideas, stretching the dimensions of the text. I am most grateful to Nissim Ezekiel and Ashish Rajadhyaksha for their minute and constructive reading of the manuscript.

Last, and first, there is my family. Many of the films I have written about are concerned with changes in family patterns, the stresses in joint family living and the traumatic shifts now taking place. For me the immediate proximity of my parents, my sister Uma and niece Kamiya has been a joy and a support that is inestimable. About my husband Sunil Roy and daughter Inca Yamini who bore with fortitude, and probably a sigh of relief, my frequent absences, mental if not physical, in the course of looking, listening, writing, I can only say that I am one of those fortunate women who has been able to combine satisfying work with the richness of a fulfilling family life.

ARUNA VASUDEV.
DELHI,
October 1986.

CONTENTS

1

POINTS OF DEPARTURE

The new Indian Cinema can be defined as variously as the creative impulses that have made it happen. It takes many shapes, from opposition to the known and the familiar, to a theoretical understanding which is different, a play with form and an excitement about structure, an attempt to find altogether a new content, and such delight in the sheer directorial thrust that both stars and stereotypes are covered in shrouds of anonymity. Sometimes a coherently structured narrative in itself is new. A film that stays within a certain genre still manages to be new, although the generic parameters of the Indian film are much more elastic than in the American, the European or the Japanese cinema. Direct or indirect criticism of the political system is new; the denunciation of casteism, feudalism, oppression, and exploitation, fear and hunger, recalls the thirties, but today helpless emotionalism has hardened into positive anger. Outward change in the Indian situation itself is reflected in new thematic concerns: the impact of cities on emigrants from the villages, political machinations, corruption, the joyous and traumatic birth of identity for the woman, the slow inevitability of change in social and personal patterns and its consequences on the individuals caught up in them.

The common denominator of most of these themes is the concern with people. No figures cast in the heroic mould; just ordinary men and women surviving under conditions sometimes of unbearable stress, surmounting their circumstances with dignity and quiet strength. It is an absolute negation of the popular cinema in which individual ambition or action has to be sacrificed to, or is motivated by, the common weal. It is a new and unfamiliar, though still tentative, process of individuation in which the alternate cinema is engaged.

The form is usually neo-realistic. Occasionally, too rarely, it trembles on the brink of poetry. The standard of craftsmanship or the theoretical comprehension is by no means uniform. The *auteur* sometimes emerges distinctly; sometimes it is the theme that takes precedence. Each director's approach and area of interest is also affected by the region in which he or she works. Films with an urban setting show a marginally greater uniformity. The commercial cinema had found that for immediate audience identification, it was simpler to give films an urban, quasi-Westernized, culturally vague background. In the new cinema, though, concerned with authenticity and specific issues, much depends on the city in which the film is set. Attitudes, dress, behaviour, relationships at every social and economic level, permeating even the relatively closer-knit, wealthy, upper-classes, differ between Bombay and Calcutta, Madras, Delhi or Hyderabad, Lucknow or Bangalore. India, to use a cliche, is a disparate, heterogeneous country which manages without noticeable psychological disruptions to live on several levels at once. And the new films reflect both its outward, sociological manifestations and the inner, psychological recesses.

In the determination to avoid the taint of "entertainment", there is a tendency to overemphasise "seriousness". The effort and the struggle show through in the first film of virtually every director. With experience and maturity, they usually acquire a greater ease of manner and a more fluid style. Through the extraordinary variety of themes, their work bears the unmistakable stamp of what is beginning to be recognised as a "Film Institute Culture". However, although in absolute figures the number of films and directors is considerable, in terms of percentage of the total production (912 films in 1985), it is infinitesimal. Yet they are the ones that earn prestige and serious critical attention; and the commercial cinema is not unaffected by it. Articulate in their views and about their objectives, they force conservative film makers into unfamiliar introspection. The effect so far can be seen in technical finish and acting style rather than in formalistic or thematic trends. Change is in the air.

It all began in the sanguine expectations raised during the post-Independence decade of the fifties in India when a fresh look was taken at the arts and the media. Determined efforts went into reviving the dying classical arts. The feudal princes and wealthy *zamindars* had been great patrons of classical music and dance. As democratic norms spelt the end of their authority, their privilege and their wealth, the very survival of the classical arts became endangered. The government took over the role of patron and preserver. For a number of years, All India Radio suspended playing film songs to concentrate on classical and authentic folk music. This helped the singers and musicians survive a difficult period, until audience taste developed sufficiently, and private cultural organisations appeared on the scene. National academies were set up to support and propagate music, dance, literature, painting, architecture and theatre. Private teaching institutions, supported frequently with government funds, independent art galleries, public performances of music and dance arranged by cultural organisations, a number of amateur theatre groups and the National School of Drama, all came up at this time.

Radio broadcasting had started in 1927; soon after 1947 its development as a national network began. An experimental television service was launched in 1959. Lack of resources for both hardware and training of personnel delayed its expansion for several years.

In the vibrant atmosphere of the 50's, the cinema began to be viewed as a possible art form. The 1951 Report of the Film Enquiry Committee constituted by the Government in 1949 to examine the state of the film industry and propose measures to further its development along desirable lines, was re-examined seriously. Cinema until this time had been treated at worst as a reprehensible, though unavoidable, social catastrophe, at best as a barbarous pastime for the uncultured. It had been allowed to go its own way, but subjected to a stern censorship and, more damagingly, to exorbitant taxation and a series of vexatious rules and regulations. No institutional financing was available. Interest rates on loans taken to make films, were prohibitively high. Despite such inhibitions, by 1960 it had become a huge industry. 319 films were made in that year alone, in 13 languages, employing several million people but there was still no infrastructure, no plans to manufacture equipment or raw film. The number of cinema houses was absurdly low (4,500 in 1960; 12,500 in 1985). Distribution and exhibition were in private hands and the motive, in view of daily increasing production costs, was profit.

It was the government itself which changed the picture when it started to implement the recommendations of the Film Enquiry Committee. In 1954, annual National Awards for excellence were introduced for directors and producers, and expanded steadily to include actors and actresses, technicians, art direction, screenplays and music. In 1960 the Film Finance Corporation was constituted (in 1980 it was amalgamated with the Motion Picture Export

Association as the National Film Development Corporation). In 1961 the Film Institute (now the Film & Television Institute of India) and in 1964 the National Film Archive, were created. With the FFC's policy decision in 1968 to start giving loans to new film-makers for "small-budget, off-beat" films, the means of production were radically expanded, and the groundwork for the arrival of an alternate cinema was laid. It was the West Bengal government's now-famous decision to assist Satyajit Ray financially to complete *Pather Panchali* which set a salutary example and, together with the film's immediate international recognition, introduced an entirely new way of thinking about the cinema. Satyajit Ray produced many of his masterpieces between 1955 and 1969. Ritwik Ghatak's emergence was equally significant as in the early sixties he made his great trilogy — *Meghe Dhaka Tara, Komal Gandhar* and *Subarnarekha*. Mrinal Sen, the third in Bengal's trinity of greats, took rather longer to arrive at a satisfying fusion of form and content. Yet outside Bengal, little had changed. The awareness that something extraordinary was taking place, made almost no impact on India's traditional cinema, well entrenched in Bombay and Madras, complacent in the knowledge that to it belonged the mass of the country's film audience. It did not feel threatened by events in far-off Bengal, nor was it stimulated by a desire to emulate them. Satyajit Ray's pre-eminence was recognised and applauded without reservation because it posed no threat. The means of production and distribution which sustained the popular cinema remained securely in place. If the pre-*Nouvelle Vague* French cinema was static, the commercial Hindi film was still more rigidly encased in its formula. Themes were limited to absurd romances interspersed with songs and dances. The average film popular in this period retained the character of a morality tale in which the glorification of poverty raises some interesting questions. It could, on the one hand, provide a validation of the Indian approach which enjoins simplicity as the true way of life. On the other, it serves a convenient purpose in sublimating dissatisfaction with economic and social inequality and stifling any tendency towards rebellion. To sustain the code yet satisfy the curiosity of audiences and the yearnings for glamour, wealth and opulence, these are shown through the life-styles of villains and vamps. The rich in cities are condemned as selfish, hedonistic, "Westernised" in their pursuit of pleasure and material gain. The hero and heroine emerge as "Indian" embodiments of goodness and simplicity, upholding all the right, traditional sentiments and principles of behaviour. Mythologicals, historicals, costume dramas, all subscribed to a basically conservative value system. The ideology of the dominant was thus perpetuated through a medium spurned by the dominant classes. The middle-class audience, attracted to the cinema by the "socials" produced by the big studios of the thirties — New Theatres in Calcutta, Bombay Talkies, Sagar Movietone and the Wadia Brothers in Bombay, Prabhat Studios in Pune — had retained some interest in the cautious social protest of a handful of directors through the next two decades who worked within the mainstream but were opposed to its ideological bias and its success formula. The end of the fifties saw the exhaustion of this small group's efforts and a further dwindling of middle-class audiences.

The uprooted working class, uneasy migrants to cities, filled the theatres.

Outside the pale of the established film industry, *Pather Panchali* aroused new hopes and determination. Slowly the conviction was born that if Satyajit Ray, an outsider, could do it, perhaps it might just be possible for others as well. A developing taste for another kind of cinema was nurtured by proliferating film societies. Echoes of the youthful spirit brushing aside the calcified, static, *"cinema de papa"* in France were heard faintly in the distance. In the winter of 1964/65, Truffaut's *The 400 Blows* and *Jules et Jim* appeared on the film society circuit in India. In 1973 the Directorate of Film Festivals was established for the purpose of organising an annual International Film Festival, while the expanding Film Society movement was actively

3

encouraged with support in specific ways. Both helped to build audiences surfeited with escapism, eager for a cinema that reflected their own traumas and pain. The struggle carried on in splended isolation by Ray, Ghatak and Sen gathered momentum, expanded across the country and, by the mid-seventies, was a movement. That it was an amorphous mass, ridden with factions, pulling in a number of opposing directions simultaneously, is immaterial. Of cardinal importance is a shared sensibility that separates it more definitively from the mainstream cinema than from antagonistic trends within it.

The strategies of the new filmmakers are divergent, the skills are uneven, but underlying them is a fascination with cinema and an abiding concern for society. There are those who believe in neo-realism as the appropriate carrier of radical messages to audiences conditioned and enculterated by the popular cinema; there are the purists who insist that radical content demands a radical form; there are still others — regrettably a minority within this minority movement — for whom cinema is the ultimate form of creative expression. Together, they have given the new Indian cinema a status held till now only by some of the other arts.

2 PRECURSORS

In all these years, the gropings towards another kind of cinema were there throughout, tentative, hesitant, never fully realised. The forces of the market place were too strong; economic imperatives and audience demand had been reduced to one and the same thing.

Formal concerns were a long way off when, in 1946, K.A. Abbas with *Dharti Ke Lal* (Children of the Earth) and Chetan Anand with *Neecha Nagar* (The Lower Depths) — with a script by Abbas, used the cinema to convey their apprehension about the direction in which society seemed to be headed. Chetan Anand adopted an allegorical form to portray the dangerously widening rift between peoples' expectations and the determination of the bourgeoisie not to recognise them. Abbas chose documentary realism for his grim tale of a peasant family caught in the great, artificially-created Bengal famine of 1943. (The food produced by the farmers was taken away by the then British government to feed its soldiers). Both films raised their funds from non-conventional sources. *Neecha Nagar* was financed by an Indian settled in England whose brother, a dancer, played the main role. *Dharti Ke Lal* was produced as a co-operative venture by the Indian Peoples' Theatre Association, the cultural wing of the Communist Party. IPTA had been formed a few years earlier with the aim of spreading social awareness through theatre. It was this Association that Ritwik Ghatak joined in 1948 and from which he went on into the cinema.

Neither of these films could be called great cinema; they are memorable principally in their opposition to the norms of the majority of their contemporaries who were steadily moving into the realm of "entertainment". Their radicalism, especially in *Dharti Ke Lal,* lay in the refusal to offer any palliatives. *Dharti Ke Lal* is stark, relentless, compelling one to face the truth. Audiences not prepared for such a harrowing test turned their backs on it. Chetan Anand succumbed, Abbas carried on undaunted. At the same time, neither of these films represents a radical departure in terms of subject matter.

More forceful in their statement and approach they provide a fitting epitaph to a tradition established in the early thirties, of films of social reform, or "socials" as they came to be known. The thirties saw a rising tide of nationalism which was reflected even in the cinema. Prevented by the censors from referring, however obliquely, to the political storm-clouds hovering over the land, they took up Mahatma Gandhi's other cry for reform within society. At that time, the means of production, in this case literally film-producing studios, were owned by thoughtful, aware individuals whose interest in the medium of cinema and involvement with the freedom struggle then coming to a head, coalesced in films with strong social messages. Audiences, too, were not yet bonded to the escapist formula. Captivated by the novelty of sound pictures, they were open to films with ideas, however simplistically expressed. It was an era of idealism, of self-examination, of hope.

By 1946, fundamental changes had taken place. Many of the studios had broken up; control over finances and distribution passed largely into the hands of commercial speculators. Audiences, seduced by the glamour of musical romances, were becoming impatient of wounding reality. The country was on the verge of Independence, but joy at this was dampened by ominous inter-communal tension which burst into large-scale violence the following year. An age of uncertainty was setting in. Films offered the only respite. Ideas were at a discount, fantasy ruled the day. Instead of becoming a conscious cultural intervention, the cinema moved with increasing determination into a fairy-tale world where dragons are slain and handsome heroes triumph against harsh parental authority — symbolising the State and social organisations — to win the beautiful maiden. With a few exceptions, this became the pattern of the popular, the only Indian cinema until the seventies. The exceptions, again, were only exceptional in their slight deviations from governing norms.

V. Shantaram's Prabhat Studios in Pune along with Bombay Talkies in Bombay and New Theatres in Calcutta. had dominated the scene in the thirties and early forties. Although his

V. Shantaram's ADMI, 1939

company folded up along with all the others, Shantaram set up another independent one, Rajkamal Kalamandir, and was able to make a few films in the earlier "social" tradition. In 1946 he based his *Dr. Kotnis Ki Amar Kahani* (The Journey of Dr. Kotnis) on K.A. Abbas's book about an Indian medical team sent to China by Nehru and the Congress Party to succour the wounded of Mao Tse Tung's Eighth Army.

Dahej (Dowry) 1950, was a fierce indictment of the largely-accepted dowry system through which families were — and to a large extent still are — compelled to raise ruinous sums to arrange opportune alliances for their daughters. The system often forces girls into disastrous marriages, sometimes with tragic consequences. *Dahej* is one of those rare films which spurn sentimentality for a suitably harsh ending. It was released at a time when the anti-dowry Bill in Parliament and in the Legislative Assemblies was under active discussion (the Prohibition of Dowry Act was passed in 1961). According to Shantaram: "When *Dahej* was released in Bihar, the members of the Legislative Assembly were inspired by my picture and I think that must have been the cause of the anti-dowry Bill being passed in the Bihar Assembly... (In Delhi) the members showed it to all the Parliamentarians and after a week or so, they introduced the Bill in Parliament and it was passed." In *Do Aankhen Baara Haath* (Two Eyes, Twelve Hands), 1957, Shantaram himself played the idealistic jailor bent on reforming six convicts held for murder. His experiment succeeds after the usual brush with an avaricious landlord. He dies, but the convicts have been reformed and are set free. Financial pressures, however, were too great to support the weight of such uneconomical ventures, despite the laurels they garnered. Shantaram settled for song and dance spectacles on the lines of his hugely popular *Jhanak Jhanak Payal Baje* (The Tinkle of Ankle Bells) in 1955.

Bimal Roy had moved to Bombay even before the closure of New Theatres in Calcutta. As a cameraman in that company, he had shot the celebrated *Devdas,* directed by P.C. Barua, which made more of an impact than any other film before or since, creating a cult around the neo-romanticism of both the character and K.L. Saigal, the actor who played him in the Hindi version. A generation is said to have wept over him as *Devdasiyat* (Devdasism) became a fashion to be cultivated. As a director in Bombay, Bimal Roy made his own version of *Devdas* with the leading players of that time, Dilip Kumar, Vyjayantimala and Suchitra Sen. More significant than *Devdas* were Bimal Roy's "socials". Extraneous events shaped his thinking. The first International Film Festival in India was held in 1952. It travelled from Delhi to Bombay, Calcutta and Madras giving Indian film-makers their first exposure to Italian neo-realism. The impact was not immediately apparent in the work of many of them but on Bimal Roy the profound impression it made was evident in his film of 1953 — *Do Bigha Zameen* (Two Acres of Land). India at that time, was a predominantly feudal, agriculture society, at a very early stage of industry and urbanisation. Many of the "socials", therefore, had a rural setting. Since most film makers, born and bred in the cities, had no direct experience of village life, their portrayals were either distorted or sentimentalized around the kernel of a hard truth. *Do Bigha Zameen,* lifted out of romanticism into genuine tragedy, is the story of a decent, hardworking peasant who, falling inevitably into debt to the powerful landowner, slowly loses everything. He moves to the city and is reduced to that most menial, humiliating and physically hazardous work of all, a rickshaw-puller. The wicked, greedy, heartless money-lender has been a constant of the Indian film. In *Damul,* made in 1984, he is still there. Unchanged.

Among Bimal Roy's other films, *Sujata* (1959) stands out for its mature technique and powerful theme although it suffers from an overwrought sensibility. Caste prejudice, a subject treated in films all through the years, was acquiring a new face under the pressure of mobility occasioned by growing industrialisation, the changing relations of production, and by legislation. In the thirties, the still-acclaimed Bombay Talkies' *Achhut Kanya* (Untouchable Girl) 1936, dared so far and no further. In it, the forbidden love between a high-caste Brahmin

Bimal Roy's DEVDAS, 1955

boy and an Untouchable girl causes them to run away together. Before they can marry, she dies. Death, or suicide has always been a convenient way out for uncomfortable situations in films. Twenty years later, in *Sujata* it was possible to arrive at a positive conclusion through a change of heart among those who opposed a marriage on grounds of caste differences.

In Mehboob Khan's *Mother India* 1957, we find the wicked landlord/money-lender again. Opposing him this time is a woman, the ideal wife, as submissive and chaste as *Sita*. The archetypal mother, she is indomitable when it comes to protecting and defending her land and the rights of her sons. The nurturing-mother role is reversed at the end and she assumes the terrifying aspect of *Kali* when she shoots down her "wicked" son. In that act, she transcends her

Nargis and Raj Kapoor in Mehboob's ANDAZ, 1949

own self, becoming in the process, the protector of the whole community against the *Adharma* of her son to emerge as the Universal Mother venerated by all. Although the film relied on many of the conventions used by the popular cinema — initial idyllic, pastoral scenes, complete with giggling maidens, a wicked and lascivious landlord, the hard struggle against a rocky, unyielding land — it moved away from a cliched presentation. The film has a clear structure corresponding to Tzvetan Todorov's definition of the ideal narrative which "begins with a stable situation which is disturbed by some power or force... There results a state of disequilibrium; by the action of a force directed in the opposite direction the equilibrium is re-established, the second equilibrium is similar to the first but the two are never identical."(*)

Its taut structure combines with strong emotional drama to grip audiences, then as now. At its periodic releases, it continues to play to full houses. There is a strong element of reassurance in its message of the rewards inherent in hard work and adherence to *dharma*.

More in line with the mainstream but with a strong undertow of socially critical comment were two films of Raj Kapoor — *Awara* (The Vagabond), 1951 and *Shree 420,* (literally "Mr. 420", the figure refers to Section 420 of the Indian Penal Code which deals with fraud) 1955. In both the scripts, written by K.A. Abbas, Raj Kapoor combines showmanship with social revolt, getting the best of all possible worlds. He believes in entertainment through emotional identification, and succeeds to an unprecedented degree. He wishes to communicate to his massive audiences a message of equality and loving kindness — and knows how to do it. It is an adroit union of serious intent and commercial viability, the envy of many of today's new film-makers striving for a similar synthesis. With Raj Kapoor it works because his stylish manner covers a genuine involvement. He came early under the influence of Abbas, and made his third film *Awara* with a script by Abbas. A rich, sophisticated, orphaned young woman lawyer lives with her adoptive father, a stern judge of the old school. A poor, orphaned young tramp brought up by a criminal is in love with her since childhood. It has all the ingredients of rich melodrama and the strands of several themes: the case for heredity over environment; the moral dilemma posed by a reference to mythology in the judge's rejection of his wife. Kidnapped and then returned home by a criminal wreaking revenge on the judge, she is just a helpless pawn. The rocky course of true love separated by class and wealth has a melodramatic resolution, with the tramp turning out to be the judge's son. These plots and sub-plots are charged with a vibrant sensuality in the scenes between Raj Kapoor and Nargis. The expressionistic dream-sequence stirred secret desires and ambitions in the viewer while the sensuously lilting music swept through the country. The appeal of the film was universal. From Bombay to Moscow, strains of the song "Awara Hoon" were heard and played over and over again. India became known as the land of Raj Kapoor and Nargis. *Shree 420,* made in 1955 (the same year as *Pather Panchali)* came close to *Awara,* without quite matching it. The tramp in both, created in Chaplin's image, has more specific connotations in *Shree 420*. It is less of a satisfying fantasy, more closely related to an unpleasant, contemporary reality. But Raj Kapoor had found his *metier* and a prominent place in the history of Indian cinema.

Abbas meanwhile, continued along his preferred path with indifferent box office success but mounting prestige, and no waning of enthusiasm for the causes he espoused. He set up his own production company, Naya Sansar, and the year after Raj Kapoor's triumph with *Awara,* Abbas made *Anhonee* (Strange Happening) with Raj Kapoor, and with Nargis playing a double role as the good and bad sisters. With *Munna* (The Lost Child), 1954 about a little boy accidentally separated from his mother, he won much acclaim for the first Hindi film without songs and dances. The splitting of the good and the bad — two brothers, two friends, two

---

* T. Todorov *The Politics of Prose* (Oxford, Blackwell 1977) p 111, quoted in John Tulloch, *The Australian Cinema* (George Allen & Unwin, 1982) pp 186-187.

sisters, the kind mother and the wicked stepmother, etc. — or the child separated from its parents by fate or by villainy were both taken up later as the starting point of a new success formula in the commercial cinema. It was Abbas who launched Amitabh Bachchan on his meteoric rise to fame, giving him a role as one of the *Saat Hindustani* (Seven Indians) 1969, with national integration as its theme. It was Abbas who made *The Naxalites,* about the movement passionately embraced by militant young activists from the late sixties onward.* New forces in society were in fact bringing in new subjects, as Brecht had said, though new forms did not creatively follow. Abbas' attempt to explore a new subject without giving it a new form was bound to fail, both critically and commercially. The Naxalite movement and its effects is the explicit or indirect subject of the work of several politically motivated new directors, each of whom tried to handle it in his own way. For them, as for Abbas, the cinema is a weapon to be used in the struggle to build a new society.

In none of the films that Abbas made himself was he able to capture the hearts and minds of audiences in the way that those he wrote for others did. *Bobby* which he wrote for Raj Kapoor in 1973 was the outstanding success of the decade. Into a story of young love and parental disapproval he wove in a plea for communal harmony and understanding.

Hrishikesh Mukherjee had been a well-established film editor in Calcutta before migrating to Bombay to join Bimal Roy's unit. "He was the only one of us who had a little money," Mrinal Sen recollects, a little enviously! The script for the first film he directed, *Musafir* (The Traveller), 1957 was written by Ritwik Ghatak. It brought a certain prestige but no success and his left-wing sympathies had to be diluted into more commercially acceptable themes and forms. In *Anuradha,* 1960, he drew a sensitive portrait of an intelligent woman's loneliness in a village where her idealistic doctor-husband chooses to practise. Her decision to leave him is sadly accepted by her husband until coincidence, chance and fate intervene to bring about understanding and reconciliation. The end may be a compromise but it is one of those rare films of the period in which the woman is the active subject, capable of taking decisions, not the passive, submissive stereotype of a wife. All his films are marked by a warm understanding of human situations and, at a technical level, a sure control over pace and rhythm. He is still much in demand as an editor while continuing to make pleasantly entertaining films around family situations — Basu Chatterjee's future territory.

Decidedly the major figure of this period was Guru Dutt, another emigrant to Bombay from Hyderabad via Calcutta and Pune. His early films are unimportant samplings of popular trends but with *Pyaasa* (Eternal Thirst) 1957, he achieved a tragic stature. In this as in *Kaagaz Ke Phool* (Paper Flowers) 1960, one senses the recognition of film as art. Both the films end in tragedy. There is liberal use of music and songs and some comedy scenes in *Pyaasa,* but by and large the central mood is sustained throughout. There is no confusion of genres, no easy concessions to popular taste. Finely controlled craftsmanship, strong characterisation and a poetic imagination, which transcends specifics of time and place, distinguish these last two films. Superficial links with *Devdas* can be seen in the poet Vijay's (played by Guru Dutt) steady sinking into alcohol, in the prostitute who falls in love with him and abandons her profession. But *Pyaasa* has a strong inner core. It never becomes maudlin or exploitative of audience susceptibilities. The poet's alcoholism is not mere self-indulgence. It stems equally from an impotent anger at the world around him. It is not a surrender to circumstances. It is a protest against them.

In this period, several poets with a background in the social commitment of the Indian Peoples' Theatre Association were persuaded to write lyrics for film songs. The Urdu poet Sahir

* To the author

11

Guru Dutt's SAHIB, BIBI AUR GHULAM, 1962

Ludhianvi wrote all the songs for Guru Dutt. Among the most memorable of these is the one in *Pyaasa* which was nearly banned by the Censor Board for its inflammatory potential: Jinhe Naaz hai Hind par woh kahan hein? (Where are they who are so proud of India?) is sung against a visual background of urban poverty and slums. Guru Dutt was tormented by a tragic view of the world. As much as Devdas, the character played by Guru Dutt in *Pyaasa* or in *Kaagaz Ke Phool,* and to some extent in *Chaudhvin Ka Chand,* is consumed by a self-destructive, depressiveness. He is a solitary existentialist, seeking a reason to live but convinced deep within him that it does not exist. The Outsider created by Barua and Guru Dutt in their own image, underwent a curious transformation in the angry rebel replicated in film after film by Amitabh Bachchan twenty years later. The Amitabh Bachchan character might be an activist, righting wrongs with the power of his fist, but underneath the violence one can sense the same lonely figure repeating the Guru Dutt refrain from *Pyaasa: yeh duniya agar mil bhi jaaye to kya hai?* (Were I to win this world what would I have gained)?

The near-nihilism of *Kaagaz Ke Phool,* seemed to reflect Guru Dutt's own life, literally and metaphorically. The film director who has lost the capacity to make films has nothing in common with Fellini's 8½. The tragic flaw in the film's main character, its elegiac mood, are not more significant than the deteriorating working conditions in the Bombay film-world of the period. The crisis was coming to a peak. Those for whom cinema was more than a marketable commodity were being edged out or forced into conforming. This was Guru Dutt's last film as a director. He continued to act, and even produced two films. Though directed, ostensibly, by others, both *Chaudhvin Ka Chand* (1960) and *Sahib, Bibi aur Ghulam* (1962) are suffused with a romantic gloom. In *Sahib, Bibi aur Ghulam* it is Meena Kumari who is the unforgettable personification of the tragic figure. Her husky voice, big, luminous eyes and ravaged beauty are in perfect consonance with the period setting of the film, which shows a rare sensitivity to the enslaving position of women, in the most exalted spheres of life as in the poorest.

Three years later Guru Dutt was dead, at thirty-nine. Accident or suicide? It was never firmly established. With him an era ended. The Bombay film industry, which set the pattern for the mainstream cinema in all languages, all regions, moved into the field of entertainment with a vengeance.

The middle-class audience attracted to the cinema by the "socials" of the thirties, had started showing signs of restiveness over the following two decades. Now it moved right away to leave the field free for a working-class mass public. The watchword became extravagance — in sets, style, fantasy, music, dance, emotion. Psychological relief was sought in escapism. Everything was exaggerated. The cinema became larger than life.

Then, in one corner of India, reality surfaced, bright and unexpected. Hope came in the form of a cinema which did not strive to deny the rigours of life but came to terms with its turmoil. It opened a whole new world for a new generation of filmmakers. In 1955, Satyajit Ray made *Pather Panchali* (The Song of the Road) in Calcutta. Perceptions of Indian cinema by outsiders and by Indians themselves have never been the same since. In Europe, the recognition was immediate, the acclaim universal. In America, it polarised critics between those who raved about it and those who, like Bosley Crowther of the New York Times, compared it sarcastically with Hollywood films — "... Any picture as loose in structure or as listless in tempo as this one would barely pass as a 'rough cut' with the editors in Hollywood." "Rough cut" or not, it ran for seven months in New York City on being released by Edward Harrison, Ray's courageous distributor. They met at the Flaherty Seminar to which *Pather Panchali* was invited. With this first film, Ray's reputation became internationally established. *Aparajito* won him the Golden Lion at Venice, and by the time *Apur Sansar* appeared, his fifth film which completed the trilogy, the encomiums were so formidable that Stanley Kauffman, who had some initial reservations about *Pather Panchali,* could write: "(the trilogy), puts him among foremost contemporary directors by reason of a general purity of vision..." Daniel Talbot, founder of the New Yorker Cinema, author of *Film: an Anthology* and generally respected for recognising films that were ahead of their times, wrote in "Progressive": "...Ray emerges in my opinion as the outstanding film artist of the new generation. He is a humanist poet, a realist, unsentimental but majestically romantic..." About *Apur Sansar* he said, "Every inch of celluloid is the work of an inspired man."(*)

In India, *Pather Panchali* made an impact that was more significant than critical acclaim. From being considered a somewhat disreputable profession practised by people of doubtful morals and behaviour, the realisation dawned upon people that cinema was an art. Indeed, great art. Even though at the time, "artists" were regarded with a sort of amused indulgence as not quite respectable "bohemians", cinema began to be taken seriously. This change in attitude did not stem so much from instant recognition of Ray's films as great art. It was inspired as much by the feeling that if someone of Ray's family and social background could actually be making films, then it may not be such a questionable activity after all. It was to cause a major change in the Government's view: to persuade it of the legitimacy of cinema, of its right to be treated on par with painting, music, dance, literature, theatre and architecture, to set up a school for its study, to support it through institutional financing, and to undertake a number of other related measures. It showed the authorities and the urban intelligentsia, what the cinema could be. *Pather Panchali*, for its cinematic qualities and the fact that it was Satyajit Ray who had made it, is the key moment in the evolution of the Indian cinema.

---

* Robert Steele, "Satyajit Ray Takes his Measure of Americans" in *Montage*, Special Issue on Satyajit Ray, No. 5/6, July 1966, Anandam Film Society, Bombay.

3

GENESIS

Between 1955 and 1969, Satyajit Ray made 15 feature films, and one full-length documentary on Rabindranath Tagore. The themes were varied, the treatment polished, the convictions humanist. The historian, Aristotle said, deals with the particular, the poet with the universal. Although Ray's films deal with specific Indian traditions—aesthetics, principles, customs, behaviour— his ultimate and overriding concern remains the *human* condition, investing his films with a poet's universality. It has been argued in India that his sensibility is European, that he is too Anglicised to be truly Indian and even less so truly Bengali; that as a distinguished member of the intellectual elite, he was self-conscious in his search for Indianness, that it did not come naturally to him as it did to his other illustrious contemporary Ritwik Ghatak. Marxists deplore his nostalgia for an ordered past, castigate him for not facing the present squarely, for his lack of anger. Others, and they are legion, point to the "little things" in his films that reveal "large truths", that films like *Jalsaghar* or *Devi* say more about upper-class decadence than tub-thumping rhetoric, that the quality of his greatness is that he sees no villains, only victims, that a little more of the compassion and generous understanding he brings to all his characters might make for a better world than violent action even for a just cause, which in the end brings devastation on the heads of the innocent and guilty alike.

Ray was a product, as it has been frequently pointed out, of the Bengal Renaissance, a nineteenth-century flowering of intellectual, artistic and political thought, synthesizing the Western scientific approach with an Indian instinctive aesthetic, bringing a rationalist spirit to bear on superstitious beliefs and fossilized social practices. Its spirit was broadly international, firmly nationalist in essence and in substance.

Ray's first film was the first in many senses : the village as a setting, signifying possibly a quest for the "real" India physically and, in a more personal sense, psychologically; neo-realism as an idiom; a cast of non-professionals; classical music composed by Ravi Shankar; a rigorous structure based on Western music, combined with a profoundly Indian sensibility characterized by a sense of wonder, the evocation of aesthetic emotion, of suggestion rather than the explicit statement.*

A pragmatist, Ray accepts that "There is not a public in India for sophisticated or subtle films. One cannot dismiss, or underestimate this fact. All producers have to keep this in mind if

---

* Wimal Dissanayake : "Art, Vision & Culture: Satyajit Ray's Apu Trilogy Revisited." Paper for 4th Hawaii International Film Symposium. 1984.

15

they wish to avoid bankruptcy. In this sense you could call me a commercial director. I have to think of audiences when I prepare a scenario. I will not accept a single compromise on the level of moral values and aesthetic forms to satisfy public taste. But I have to remember the intellectual co-efficient of the audience. I consider myself responsible to the producer who risks his money on my film; I would not want him to lose his capital because of me. So I try always to be as economical as possible within my framework."*

Ray has often been likened in his humanism to Jean Renoir. He agrees. "Renoir is one of the cineastes I admire enormously," although he also learnt a great deal from Billy Wilder and William Wyler and John Ford, about "the fundamentals of editing, camera positions, etc.".... But, he adds, "A film-maker is not necessarily influenced only by other cineastes. He can be influenced by writers and by photographs. I was greatly influenced by Cartier-Bresson and by Indian literature."**

The influences are diverse but they have been internalised. What results is a cinema that bears Ray's very personal stamp. A limpid flowing anecdote and always, a commitment which goes beyond narrow party politics or dogma to moral values. To society rather than systems. He looks at the world with affectionate irony, never transgressing the limits of restraint he imposes upon himself and demands from his characters. The discourse is so human, so universal, that no code is required to decipher it. On the surface, his films appear simple, unaffected, easy. But the ease comes from perfect control. Ray never wants to dazzle with technical daring. His technique lies in the whole beautifully balanced structure of the film.

Which is not to say that he never falters. Each film cannot be a masterpiece. But he has produced more of them than his fair share. Before 1969 he had made, apart from the Apu trilogy, *Jalsaghar* (The Music Room), *Devi* (The Goddess), *Teen Kanya* (Three Daughters). *Kanchenjunga, Mahanagar* (The Big City), and the film he considers his best, *Charulata*. It was the apogee of an extraordinarily rich period. *Charulata* is quintessential Ray. Charulata herself is one of the most sensitive, intelligent, emotionally strong and memorable women to reach the Indian screen. She stands out even among Ray's films in which the women are invariably complex, subtle, strong individuals. "What I admire in women is grace, sophistication, intelligence," he has said. And that "the beauty of a woman like Charulata is largely the beauty of her mind. What I've tried to bring out in the film is the richness of that mind. That comes out through her responses to the world and especially through her growing attachment to Amal, her young brother-in-law. Its an illicit relationship but it's beautiful since it reveals the nuances of a sensitive person."*** And through the nuances of Ray's technique. His care for the evocative detail, in images as in sound; in *Charulata* the swing, the floral motifs, the Victorian-Indian style of dressing; the look in Charulata's eyes which expresses greater depth than words can convey. In *Mahanagar,* the scene where Aditi tries on lipstick for the first time, timidly, marvelling at her own temerity. That small gesture holds within it the nascence of a transformation in her which in turn implies the cataclysmic transformation in social and family relationships, just beginning to shake the foundations of ancient traditions. The end of the film is a little simplistic with the husband and wife jobless, but together in spirit after a period of hurt and refusal to understand each other. The optimism seems misplaced in view of the reality with which they had to cope.

With every film, Ray was reaffirming his mastery, in a continuous flowing line. Suddenly, with *Kapurush-o-Mahapurush* (The Coward and the Holy Man), 1965, which followed

* Satyajit Ray, An Anthology of Statements on Ray by Ray, ed. C.D.G., D.N. of FF. New Delhi 1981
** Henri Micciolo. *Satyajit Ray*. Editions L'Age d'Homme, Paris, 1981 p. 247
*** H. Micciolo, *op. cit,* pp 250-251.

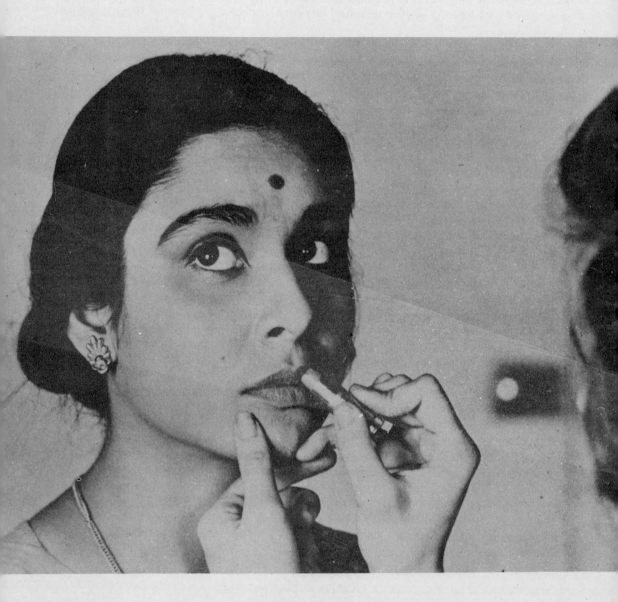

Satyajit Ray's MAHANAGAR. 1963

Charulata, the momentum stops. According to Chidananda Das Gupta, "it marks the beginning of a phase of spiritual exhaustion after a series of magnificent and masterly works. It is as if he had finished all he had to say."* *Nayak* (The Hero) 1966 has some weaknesses one could never have suspected, judging by the films that preceded it, an expressionism that is surprising. In it are the hints of the pessimism that was to invade Ray's later work. Each film-maker at some stage in his life, seems to feel a compulsion to make one film on his medium. This is Ray's. But it is not a film on the cinema as, for example, *Kaagaz Ke Phool* or Truffaut's *Day for Night.* It is a psychological study of a successful actor. The portrait of the Star, the fanfare, the glamour, the hero worship that surrounds him and which, for him, passes for reality, is skilfully constructed and then picked apart to reveal the torment and the emptiness inside. Appearance and reality, the anguish that lies behind the image, the fake dreams given the lie by the real dream. For the first time, one feels Ray's lack of sympathy with the main character, despite his best efforts to understand him. "It is a film about different levels of exploitation in a capitalist society, even though each one has its own reasons for existence,"* Ray said about it. With *Chiriakhana* (The Menagerie), 1967, which followed, Ray reached the lowest point of his work. He seemed drained of energy. External forces added to it. Hollywood called. He planned to make a film in English *The Alien,* with Peter Sellers. Science fiction is a genre that has always interested him, and going into an area so completely different from anything he had worked in earlier might have restored his flagging spirit. Columbia was supposed to finance it but plans fell through after nearly a year's negotiations. At home, his producer had problems as absurd as anything that might be imagined. One of the bank notes he had printed for the dream sequence in *Nayak* was discovered by someone who tried to pass it off for real. The producer, on whose head it rebounded, was accused of printing false money. The affair was ridiculous and soon blew over. But the Bengali cinema was in a period of crisis. The producer A.D. Bansal with whom Ray had a close association since Mahanagar, decided to invest in Hindi films. Ray found himself in a financial position as precarious as when he started working on *Pather Panchali.*

All this time, Ray had been looked up to as the one single hope of Indian cinema. He had been lauded, given awards, studied by hopeful film-makers who were inspired by his "new language of film"** Even the commercial film-world of Bombay, without wishing to emulate him, even if they could, held him in awe. But now murmurs of disapproval began to be heard. Why didn't he show a greater concern with the world around him? The "Calcutta of the burning trains, communal riots, refugees, unemployment, rising prices and food shortages"* was never seen in any of his films. At the Film Institute, Ritwik Ghatak had been Vice Principal for five critical months in 1965, and his band of loyal disciples began the debate between the work of these two entirely different directors, comparing Ray unfavourably with Ghatak. Ray's reserve and aloofness were contrasted with Ghatak's accessibility as he drank and joked with his students at the Institute and with the young Marxists who gathered around him. Ghatak's films, less well-known internationally and nationally at this time, were deeply admired by small groups who found in them echoes of the malaise they experienced, as well as a technique and a concern they felt were of more immediate significance. Mrinal Sen too had started making films which openly attacked the system as it was emerging. With *Bhuvan Shome,* 1969, Sen arrived with a bang on the national scene.

Ray's humanism and moral values seemed to belong to a calmer world of order and idealism. The India of the Tagore-Nehru era was being pushed out by a harsher, shriller, tension-ridden

* Chidananda Das Gupta : *The Cinema of Satyajit Ray.* Vikas Publishing, New Delhi, 1980, p. 41.
* Henri Micciolo, *op cit.* page 299
** See page (Aravindan)
* Chidananda Das Gupta, *The Cinema of Satyajit Ray, op cit* p 44.

reality. Ray retreated from it into musical fantasy with *Goopy Gyne Bagha Byne* (The Adventures of Goopy and Bagha) 1968, back to a sense of wonder. It was something he was to keep returning to in the next twelve years as a kind of talisman to keep faith alive and stress at bay. *Goopy Gyne Bagha Byne* is based on a story by his grandfather Upendrakishore Roychowdhury, one of the many he wrote for children among his other activities. It gave Ray the chance to experiment with technique—and music. It has magic and special effects—the dance of the ghosts is brilliantly done—plenty of songs, and music which he himself composed. He had been composing his own music ever since *Teen Kanya*, but in *Goopy Gyne* he gave full rein to his own musical talent. It has everything to delight children, and adults who have managed to retain some sense of innocence. But, as Ray said wryly in an interview, "of course the scenario also includes a tyrannical king, corrupt ministers, brainwashing. You see.... very contemporary themes."

Almost in spite of himself, Ray was being pushed by the fever and fret around him into the kind of "progressive" attitude that many expected and some demanded of him. But he had to come to it in his own way and in his own time.

Goopy seemed to have acted as a tonic. The next year he made *Aranyer Din Ratri* (Days and Nights in the Forest), one of the films that he himself prefers, and it is unquestionably among his greatest works. It signifies the beginning of his move into contemporary Calcutta — at one remove. Four friends leave the city to spend a few days in the forest. In their encounter with nature, with the three women they meet, their arrogant indifference to others, we see them awakening to a sense of responsibility, externally, and to an uneasy awareness of their own selves, internally. It has been called "Chekhovian", "Mozartian". It led Pauline Kael to one of the greatest tributes to any director: "No artist has done more than Satyajit Ray to make us re-evaluate the commonplace."* And Stuart Byron noted that, "For all its behavioural charm and comedy, *Days and Nights in the Forest* is one of the most despairing films ever made...." It is certainly one of Ray's most disturbing films, reflecting perhaps his own state of mind at this time. Calcutta was present, waiting in the wings, and had to be faced. The days and the nights in the forest were a bitter-sweet overture. Its density is a far cry from the simplicity of *Pather Panchali*, even from *Charulata*. Perhaps Ray himself was beginning to feel the need to reflect the troubled world outside in the troubled minds of his characters.

In the same year as *Aranyer Din Ratri* Ray started his trilogy on Calcutta with *Pratidwandi* (The Adversary) continued with *Seemabaddha* (Company Limited) in 1971 and closed four years later with *Jana Aranya* (The Middleman). Through the three films, Calcutta takes shape, warts and all. The seaminess, the struggle for jobs, the idealism that takes the form of protest as the young join the Naxalite movement, the loss of innocence in *Jana Aranya* as integrity settles for pragmatism. The old father alone reminds us of the moral values of an earlier age.** Ray sees that the young have few choices. Survival means compromise; defiance and the pursuit of idealism means opting for the violence of revolutionary action. Ray wants to bring to them his own innate compassion but cannot avoid the tinge of pessimism. It is not a world he can like. And his usual understanding takes on a certain analytical coldness. The shooting style changes accordingly, from slow movements and long beautifully-controlled takes into abrupt cuts, hand-held shots, getting closer into the action, trying to find a core of truth and pain under the surface shrewdness.

The present had rubbed off on the past, for after *Seemabaddha* Ray made *Ashani Sanket* (Distant Thunder) where the equilibrium of an ordered scheme of things is upset by destructive

---

* Pauline Kael, *The New Yorker* 1973 quoted in *Satyajit Ray* ed. Chidananda Das Gupta, Directorate of Film Festivals, New Delhi, 1980, p. 81

** Saeed Mirza suggests a similar faith in the strong moral fibre of the "Independence generation" in his *Mohan Joshi Hazir Ho*. See pp. 109-110.

external forces: the (British) man-made famine which was the subject of Abbas' *Dharti Ke Lal* and of Mrinal Sen's *Baishey Shravan* (The Wedding Day) 1960. The thunder of war is far away, but in a small village people die of hunger as the food they produce goes to sustain the army. The colour in which the film is shot, the lush, lovely landscape, make death all the more horrifying. Compassion for the characters, a finely controlled anger for the false destiny over which they have no control: it could be today.

The world was too much with Ray and he returned to another of his delightful children's films before embarking on the last of his city films. *Sonar Kella* (The Golden Fortress) 1974 combines fantasy with the mystery genre in Ray's own story. Felunath, his detective, reappears later in *Joi Baba Felunath* (The Elephant God) in 1979.

In *Shatranj Ke Khilari* (The Chess Players) 1977 Ray makes his first, and only foray outside Bengal. In *Ashani Sanket* the British are behind the famine in a Bengal village which is responsible for physical deaths. In *Shatranj*, it is again the British, in an earlier period, who try to destroy the moral strength of Indians at the top of the social and economic scale as they tighten their grip on the country. The film has a scheme that is brilliantly conceived. The distribution of colour, the movements of the two chess players on the chess board, a metaphor for the real movements as the Nawab of Avadh faces the power of the British in the form of General Outram, the sense of an eternal India that has suffered invasions and conquests and survived by absorbing them. It is a beautiful inversion of power where the seemingly strong succumb before the inner strength of the seemingly weak. As Henri Micciolo points out in his book*, "Outram senses that he is committing an injustice which dishonours him, the King (of Avadh) is capable of true grandeur ... It is not far from *Seemabaddha* where the apparent victor is the real loser." That, Satyajit Ray agreed, was his own intention.** It gives his film a resonance and, yes, a much more profound humanity than an external, essentially simple, though vast battle for power.

Shatranj ke Khilari was produced by Suresh Jindal, another independent producer who believed, like Shashi Kapoor, in good cinema that could also be financially viable. He had earlier produced Basu Chatterji's most successful film *Rajnigandha* and was later to do Sai Paranjpye's *Katha*. From his student days at the University of California, Los Angeles, he had admired Satyajit Ray. The unexpected financial bonanza of *Rajnigandha* gave him the opportunity and the courage to approach Ray with an offer. "I was hoping he would be interested in a Hindi film, or, if not, then perhaps English. And if not either of those languages, I would have accepted Bengali. Whatever he wanted would have been alright with me," Jindal said. But Ray had been thinking of Hindi and had, in fact, a story of Premchand in mind when Suresh Jindal came to him in Calcutta with his proposal. The Hindi film world was aghast at Satyajit Ray's entry into its territory. Distribution was beset by artificially created problems and controversy, distasteful to the quiet, reserved Satyajit Ray. He plunged back into refreshing, cleansing musical fantasy, back into Bengali, and produced in quick succession *Joi Baba Felunath* and *Hirok Rajar Deshe* (The Kingdom of Diamonds), a sequel to *Goopy Gyne Bagha Byne*. A short film *Pikoo's Day,* for French Television, and Ray was at last able to make the film he had planned even before *Pather Panchali, Ghare Baire* (Home and the World), based on the famous novel of Rabindranath Tagore. It is the turn of the century, the period with which Ray feels such affinity and in which he had placed another of his great films, *Charulata,* also on a novel of Tagore's. In the years since *Charulata,* Ray had changed. *Charulata*'s exquisite lightness made way for a heavier, more sombre tone. Its scope is wider. Under the three-way relationship of Bimala, Nikhil and Sandip sounds the muffled beat of history.

---

* Henri Micciolo — *Satyajit Ray, op cit* page 317

** In 1978 Shyam Benegal made *Junoon* with the Indo-British conflict as the background. See page 41

Individual actions and emotions spring from attitudes towards nationalist causes. Bimala, Nikhil's wife, is attracted to Sandip the activist. Nikhil's detachment and apparent inactivity springs from a profound dedication to moral values that reflect Ray's own. But she cannot see it. For Sandip the ends justify the means. In him are the seeds of the ethical disintegration which grew in the next decades. Bimala, urged into a realisation of herself by Nikhil's prompting, overreacts. In her newly discovered freedom, she breaks the restraint symptomatic of Ray's other women. Though deeply distressed, Nikhil remains true to his values. He waits. Sandip exposes his baseness. Bimala finally understands Nikhil's rectitude. To encapsulate that film in a few lines is to do it less than justice. It is so full of nuances, allusions, of fleeting moments charged with infinite complexity.

It is Ray's most recent film. It shows him at the acme of his creative power.

Ritwik Ghatak, Mrinal Sen and Satyajit Ray started making films within a few years of each other. Ghatak's *Nagarik* in fact predates *Pather Panchali* by three years. It is difficult to imagine three directors more different. Ray is the aristocratic product of an intellectual and artistic family in a Bengal that subsumed the classical culture of the East and the West. His cinema is sophisticated, subtle, committed to a universal humanity that transcends barriers. Ghatak, on the other hand, is deeply steeped in Indian culture, classical and popular. Marxism is his political philosophy. His Indian point of reference is the primitive culture that predates the classical; his desire, to arrive at an immediate understanding with a specifically Indian audience possessed of the necessary codes to decipher meaning fully. When *Pather Panchali* was shown at Cannes in 1956, immediate understanding followed after people realised that what they had passed up was not anywhere near the usual song-and-dance Indian extravaganza

Ritwik Ghatak on location of SUBARNAREKHA, 1962

which they had expected. The Jury gave it the award for the "Best Human Document". The rest is history.

When Ghatak's *Ajantrik, Meghe Dhaka Tara* and *Subarnarekha* were first screened in Paris at the Cinematheque Francaise in 1969, people shuffled and whispered and walked out. They were not prepared to accept melodrama, situations and relationships so specific and so distant from their own normal experience. Of course, it was also the height of the *Nouvelle Vague* in France, and perceptions of cinema were undergoing a sea change. Today Ghatak is being hailed as a master. The world has shrunk, there is a greater openness, a willingness to meet the new and the unfamiliar half-way. Ghatak's specificity is not alienating, it is challenging intellectually and welcome cinematically. He uses melodrama in a manner that is unique. It bears no similarity either to the Western cinema or to the commercial Indian cinema. It is much closer to early Indian forms of dramatic expression but used in a highly sophisticated manner and context. He is aggressive about its use in his films. "When I elaborate a story to express an idea I am not afraid to use any amount of coincidence if necessary. And I am not deterred by melodrama at all. Melodrama is a birthright, a form."* And he uses it consciously, very deliberately, to arrive at an equation with an Indian audience with whom he wished very definitely to communicate. When he adopted cinema as his medium it was not for love of cinema *per se,* as it was with Satyajit Ray. He said it himself: "When I thought of the cinema I thought of the millions of minds I could reach at the same time. This is how I came into films; not because I wanted to make films. Tomorrow if I could find a better medium I would throw away the cinema. I don't love films ... I have used the cinema as a weapon, as a medium to express my views ... and to educate people."**

One cannot take Ghatak's pronouncements too literally. There is often a curious split between what one says, arising from what one wishes to believe, and what one expresses instinctively. What Ghatak did with the materials of cinema shows that despite his professions to the contrary, he used the cinema with an understanding born of love. It was through the medium of the cinema that he was able to express his umbilical attachment to the large open spaces and waters of the Bengal he loved so well. The extreme wide-angle lens and the big screen which reveal them are the stuff of cinema alone. Theatre, with which he started, could not capture it, nor television to which those who knew him say he was attracted. The deep-focus photography, the placing of characters within the frame, the *mise-en-scene* with its novel use of space and volume, the variations in the pitch and tone of the sound track used to such controlled effect to counterpoint, not harmonise with the image, are essential Ghatak and essentially cinema.

His political allegiance came from a deep distress over the immediate problems that confronted those turned into refugees by external events. His own family was driven out of East Pakistan (now Bangladesh) when the partition of India divided Bengal in two. The sense of loss and uprooting he experienced influences most of his work. Calcutta bore the weight of millions of refugees, witnessed their pain, was powerless to afford more than marginal relief. A political consciousness among writers and artists was inevitable. The Progressive Writers Association, an anti-fascist league, had been created in Lucknow in 1936. It led to the founding of the Indian Peoples Theatre Association in 1943. The aim was to take art out of the confines of the middle class to the people, and in Calcutta it became a significant voice of protest. Ghatak became a member. He realised that the short stories he had been writing could reach only a few hundred. Audiences for IPTA's theatrical performances could be counted in the thousand. He wrote, acted, directed plays but fell out with party directives demanding clear distinctions between

* *Ritwik Ghatak,* ed. Shampa Banerjee, Directorate of Film Festivals, New Delhi, 1982 pp. 95-96.
** *Ritwik Ghatak op cit,* p. 8

23

good and evil. When IPTA decided to extend its sphere of communication beyond theatre to film. K.A. Abbas, a member of its Bombay group, was asked to make the first one. *Dharti ke Lal,* in 1946 spurred an interest in the medium. **Ghatak, Mrinal Sen and others,** plunged into reading Eisenstein and Pudovkin, Roger Manville, **Rotha and Kracauer.** "What was of prime importance was to develop a serious attitude towards cinema." They wrote scripts, worked out budgets, carried them around in their pockets. At this time, their opportunities for seeing films were limited. "The Film society had been showing good films but we had no money to join it," Mrinal Sen says. "Bansi Chandragupta (the great art director of later years) occasionally managed to take us. He had no money either but he knew Satyajit Ray and Chidananda Das Gupta" (its founder-members). *Pather Panchali,* made shortly afterwards, "gave us an emotional kick and the impetus to go the way of Ray."

1951-52 were significant years. Pudovkin and Cherkassov came to India as part of a Russian delegation. Ghatak and Sen were among those who held long discussions with them. Their reading on cinema had acquired depth and perception and the first International Film Festival in 1952 gave them a concentrated dose of seeing contemporary cinema.

Ghatak said about it later: "I am absolutely convinced of the tremendous impact the Festival had on all of us — countless films and a rare occasion for exchange of ideas. The courage and strength I derived from the Festival was translated into my unreleased film *Nagarik* (The Citizen). The transition got wonderfully articulated in *Pather Panchali.'*

Nagarik 1952 was a collective effort in which everyone including the laboratory and studio participated. The raw stock, too, was a gift. The film was not only never released, it vanished mysteriously to reappear only twenty-five years later. The theme is obviously political, the acting style and movement somewhat theatrical. But in the lighting, framing and composition of shots, it is a foretaste of the uniquely personal idiom he was to fashion so well over the next few films.

In *Ajantrik* (variously translated as The Mechanical Man or The Pathetic Fallacy, its literal meaning is "unmechanical") made six years later, Ghatak first used the extremely wide-angle lens to bring nature to life. In this enchanting relationship of a taxi driver with his old jalopy, the car has a life of its own: it sulks, it has fits of jealousy, it is gay and annoyed by turns as the film, in a series of episodes, takes us through sweeping landscapes where the individual becomes one with his environment. Each episode has a coda where Bimal goes off alone with Jagaddal (the name he has given his car) to share with "her" his exultation in the land and the waters he loves. Many of Ghatak's recognizable motifs are present: the clash of the coming mechanical age with tribal culture and tradition, the figure of the madman, the primitive, who alone can speak the truth, ending, as all his subsequent films were to do, with the image of a child, the symbol of hope, continuity, survival. *Bari Theke Paliye* (The Runaway) 1959 is an entire film about a child. A runaway who has a series of adventures in Calcutta and eventually returns chastened to his parents, happy to be home again. The film's real protagonist is the street vendor, a jobless teacher making a living as a street magician, who becomes his friend and who succeeds in persuading him to go back home. It is he who embodies Ghatak's feelings about the city with warmth and a poignant charm, he who is the motherless, homeless refugee. Ghatak's great, all-too-brief creative period was just starting. In quick succession, in three consecutive years, he made *Meghe Dhaka Tara, Komal Gandhar* and *Subarnarekha,* which might be considered his trilogy, encompassing his art and his philosophy. He had come early under the influence of Marxism, which was to form the ideological base of his films. Through Jung, the poetry of Yeats and Eric Neumann's book on comparative religions and the Great Mother, he understood and articulated his own feelings about the early, Indian tribal mother-goddess cult.

* Ritwik Ghatak, ed. Shampa Banerjee. Directorate of Film Festivals, New Delhi, 1982 pp. 95-96.
** Ritwik Ghatak, op. cit. p. 8

His considerable understanding of traditional culture was deepened and broadened by the experience gained while shooting a documentary about the Oraon tribals (in Orissa) in 1955. Repeated allusions to Indian mythology give his films a density for Indian audiences, an impenetrable quality for those unaware of them. "If you want to preach a social message you can't do without mythology," Ghatak said and believed. But mythology internalised, never obvious, never used only for simple identification. Melodrama and the epic structure are the forms within which he chose to work. The epic tradition "has seeped into the Indian unconscious. It is no surprise that Indians are attracted to mythologicals. I am a part of it... In my films I rely mainly on the folk form. The Great-Mother image in its duality exists in every aspect of our being.*

Archetypes, the collective unconscious and the Mother Goddess, myth and mythology, are recurring threads through Ghatak's last few films, from *Meghe Dhaka Tara* (Cloud-Capped Star) 1960, to *Jukti, Takko Ar Gappo* (The Story and the Argument) 1974.

Meghe Dhaka Tara, Komal Gandhar and *Subarnarekha* are singular in the wealth of their allusiveness. On a superficial level, straight narrative, they have sublime moments when Ghatak seems to touch "the threshold of the unknown". In brilliant juxtapositions of image, sound and music, one hears the resonances of his social, political and philosophical argument. It has been

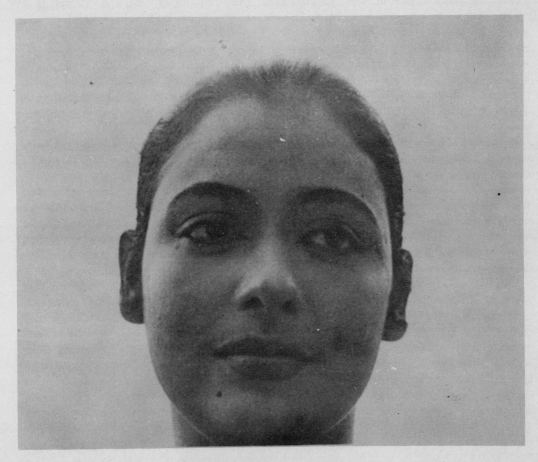

Ritwik Ghatak's KOMAL GANDHAR, 1961

* Shampa Banerjee, *op cit* p. 99.

said of Ghatak that he was an "intuitive" film-maker unconsciously achieving his effects. On the contrary, it is clear that he knew exactly what he was doing, and the improvisation emerged out of a sure knowledge of what would be just right for him and his film.

In *Meghe Dhaka Tara,* the magnificent long shot of the huge, spreading tree with which the film opens, the brother practising singing under its wide leafy branches, reappears repeatedly. It is under this tree that Sanat waits, hoping to see Neeta after he has married her younger sister. It is here that she walks away, enveloped by her big, black umbrella, leaving him stricken with remorse to the sound of the whiplash on the soundtrack. It is a brilliant counterpoint to the first time that sound is heard when Neeta stumbles down the stairs from Sanat's flat, having understood that he had betrayed her for her sister. In *Subarnarekha,*the "new home" (the idea of a new home to replace the one lost, is constantly underlined) that Sita and her elder brother move to, is the opposite of what they had been led to believe. Instead of a green, verdant land full of "flowers and butterflies", it is bare, stark, dry, rocky, harsh. When Sita and her adoptive brother discover their love, for the first time the background is a graceful forest. A sweeping 180 degree pan dissolves into another along a serenely flowing river. The effect is one of ineffable harmony. The land, for Ghatak, represented the Mother, water was *Narayana.* Together they had limitless power to soothe and to heal.

Ten years were to pass between *Subarnarekha,* 1962 (released in 1965) and the making of *Titash Ekti Nadir Naam* (A River Named Titash) in Bangladesh in 1973. In those intervening years, Ghatak made some short films, started a feature that was abandoned after a week's shooting, lectured at the Film Institute where he was Vice-Principal for five months, crucial for those students who were to be so deeply influenced by him. Alcoholism was taking hold as was a deeply growing anger over the shape of socio-political conditions, and despair at the lack of finances for film-making. In 1963, his proposal for a feature film *Aranyak,* based on a story by Bibhuti Bhushan Bandopadhyay (author of what was to become the Apu trilogy), was turned down by the Film Finance Corporation for lack of a guarantor.

Audiences too, were not responding in the way Ghatak hoped they would. "I feel alcohol is the final road to salvation," he said at the time. "I get engrossed in it. I really do."[1] He started shooting a film on Mrs. Gandhi. "I want to bring out the loneliness of the lady and I'll do it through close-ups of her hands," he planned. But alcohol was taking over. Mrs. Gandhi, who had known him over the years, also tried to persuade him to give up drinking: "I'll promise you anything if you do," she reportedly said "Alright, *didi,*" (elder sister), he agreed, and said he would be there the next morning at six. He arrived at ten-thirty in the usual cloud of alcohol. When she smiled and said, "So you couldn't do it," he was indignant. "I did come at six," he said, "but I was absolutely sober and at your gate they refused to believe I was Ritwik Ghatak."*

The film was never completed. The stories about his drinking multiplied. But films kept taking shape in Ghatak's mind. He was slowly working towards an unequivocally epic form, which finally emerged in *Titash Ekti Nadir Naam.* Bangladesh gave him the opportunity denied him at home. For Ghatak, Bangladesh was a return to his real home, the loss of which had filled his mind and his films through these long years. His health broke down completely as he finished shooting. He had to be taken back to Calcutta. The film was edited according to his instructions, but he was far from satisfied. He did go back and re-edit it later but that is not the version generally screened. However, the essential elements come through clearly. The film has an epic sweep and grandeur, the canvas is wider, the scope more ambitious than in his earlier films, the imagery so dense that it conceals as much as it reveals of his deepest concerns. The

---

* Incident recounted by his assistant Mahendra Kumar, to the author.

child's vision of his dead mother as *Bhagabati,* the goddess, the dance of the tribals, the rich sound track and the final, poignant scene where the dying heroine claws at the sandy bed of the dried river-bed to extract in vain a few drops of water. As always with Ghatak, the despair turns to hope in the last shot as a child playing a leaf whistle comes dancing through the fields. Hope, continuity, survival.

In his last film finished shortly before his death, *Jukti Takko Ar Gappo,* Ghatak looks back ruefully, ironically, on his life. Corrosively honest — how many film makers could see themselves with such brutal clarity? — it still has a measure of optimism. Society has collapsed, the intellectual is at sea, political idealism has been wounded by grim political reality. But Ghatak keeps intact his faith in the individual, in truth, in hope. Playing himself in his autobiographical film, his dying words are: "Something has to be done."

Ghatak never really succeeded in communicating in any significant manner with the audience. *Meghe Dhaka Tara* was the only one of his films that connected immediately. He died at fifty in 1976. He died of frustration, of anger, of alcohol, of a fire that burned too brightly. Saeed Mirza once asked him about the test of a good director. The answer was typical Ghatak — "In one pocket a bottle of liquor, in the other your childhood."

Mrinal Sen's boundless energy and enthusiasm are reflected in the films he makes. The eclecticism of his subjects and the variety of their languages — Bengali, Oriya, Telugu and Hindi — are an indication of his own inquiring, restless, iconoclastic and always youthful spirit. Mrinal Sen shows no signs of ageing. But he has mellowed. And so have his films. The growth of the man is paralleled in his films from the first "very bad" (his words) *Raat Bhore* (Night's End) in 1956, through the middle period when he took to flag-waving propaganda, to the grace and warm perceptiveness of the last few films. From dialectical Marxism to a humanist philosophy: it is a 22-film voyage of fits and starts to an unclear destination. One cannot say of each film, as one can of Ray's or Ghatak's, that it is "unmistakably Sen". With *Pather Panchali* Ray emerged as it were, like Athena from the brow of Zeus, fully armed. With Sen, the birth and the maturing were a slow, painful process. The hand of the *auteur* is not distinct. However, from the start to the present, the *corpus* of the work reveals a fascinating evolution, in the man, in society, in the film-maker, and in the shape of Indian cinema itself.

Raat Bhore was an unsatisfying experience, *Neél Akasher Neechay* (Under the Blue Sky) had a slightly stronger, more political stance, but it was *Baishey Shravana* (A Wedding Day) 1960 that first brought all Sen's thoughts on cinema together. He had been strongly affected by *Dharti Ke Lal* and by a Bengali film *Chinnamool* made shortly afterwards by Nemai Ghosh about the refugees who fled from East Bengal (now Bangladesh) to India after the partition of the country. He was not personally touched by the partition of Bengal, like Ghatak. His concern was for the larger cause of all who suffer. *Baishey Shravana* is a tender love story that grows out of marriage and its bitter end in the famine that stalked the land. "I wanted to show the ugliness, the cruelty, the implacable nature of famine," he said. He did. But he also revealed the humanity that refused to surrender. The black and white photography has a fifties look about it, but Sen's technique is confident. As a film maker he had arrived.

Over the next three films, Sen tried out variations on the theme of marriage in an urban middle-class milieu. In *Punascha* (Over Again) the wife starts to work — and the problems arise. *Abasheshey* (And at Last...) is a comedy on divorce, *Pratinidhi* (The Misfits) a tragedy on a marriage frowned upon by society. In two of the themes he took up — *Baishey Shravana* and *Punascha* — he pre-empted Satyajit Ray's *Ashani Sanket* and *Mahanagar* but the attitudes are poles apart. Sen the realist chooses to look squarely at the situation, Ray the aesthete and the humanist prefers to suggest it through reactions to it.

Mrinal Sen, interview with Michel Ciment, *Positif 250* Paris, January 1982, p. 64

Mrinal Sen's EK DIN PRATIDIN. 1979

With *Akash Kusum* (The Daydream) in 1956, Mrinal Sen's delight in the medium of cinema soared. He saw *Jules et Jim* and was introduced to the French *Nouvelle Vague* at a film society screening in Bombay early in 1965. Eisenstein and Pudovkin, *Rome, Open City* and *Miracle in Milan* were forgotten in the excitement of the medium, the infinite variations of style possible. He put away conventional narrative to start out on a period of experimentation. Jump cuts, freeze frames, it was as if he had just discovered special effects and wanted to try them all out. The breezy style of the film did not prevent Sen from making "a serious socio-economic point", as he said. He and his scenarist Ashish Barman refused the easy sentimentality of a happy ending which they felt would have been "unconvincing and hence disastrous". Their stress on the "topicality" of the film led to a three-cornered two-month debate in a national daily between Barman, Satyajit Ray and Mrinal Sen with fifty or so others joining it. As Sen writes, "it was funny, intriguing and perhaps important too." It also shows that Satyajit Ray was not as aloof or withdrawn from intellectual and artistic battles as he has been made out to be. The correspondence throws light on the wit, the knowledge of cinema and the literary background of the participants. It also made their positions clear. Sen departed, bloody but unbowed, for fresh fields. He made *Matira Manisha* (Two Brothers) in Oriya. Why? Because it is challenging to work in a milieu and a language not your own. It forces you to extend yourself, and yet "the culture of poverty is the same all over the world; exploitation follows a certain ubiquitous pattern," as he says. An ordinary family drama becomes a valid social document. Its incidental but significant benefit was to give a boost to film-making in Orissa.

Sen had now made eight films. Their extremely low budgets allowed him to continue working out his ideas, polishing his craft and his film language. It did not suit him temperamentally to be restricted to a single region because of the language. He decided to apply to the Film Finance Corporation for a film to be made in Hindi. The result was *Bhuvan Shome* — as significant a step in Sen's own evolution as in that of the emergence of an alternate cinema.

From the sombre tones of his "social documents" Sen moved out into a lighter, gayer atmosphere, literally and figuratively. The stern bureaucrat moves out of his austere office into a sunlit landscape, and encounters an impudent village girl who has never known what it means to be confined. As irresistibly as a magnet she draws out his inhibitions, his pretensions. He sheds them as unresistingly as he discards his constricting coat and tie for the freedom of the loose Indian *kurta pyjama*. It might also be a metaphor for the Indian film, moving out from the stuffiness of studios and mannered acting, away from the persistent Hollywood influence, into a saner, fresher, *younger* world, as also the beginning of a search for an idiom more relevant to a contemporary Indian sensibility. The inspiration was "Truffaut's youthfulness" and Jacques Tati's "inspired nonsense". It also evoked a tongue-in-cheek summary by Satyajit Ray in the seven words considered by Hollywood to be the criterion for a good screen story — "Big Bad Bureaucrat Reformed by Rustic Belle."[*] It shows Sen in a happy, carefree mood although the apparent stylistic improvisation is undoubtedly carefully planned. He followed it with a one-hour comedy for children *Ichchapuran* (Wish Fulfilment) based on a Tagore story, and then returned to his initial and continuing preoccupation — the aesthetics of violence in the unholy alliance between poverty and politics. During this period (early seventies), he wrote, "I have of late developed a taste for pamphleteering to blend the fictional with the actualities, to draw conclusions on a propagandist note...this is my area of experimentation. This is where I am now trying to discover myself."[**]

Interview, Calcutta 71, Padatik (The Guerilla Fighter), *Chorus,* followed each other in quick succession. The daily, deteriorating grind in Calcutta magnified by social, economic and

[*] Satyajit Ray, *Our Films Their Films*, Orient Longman Ltd., 1976, p. 99
[**] Mrinal Sen, *Views on Cinema*, Ishan, Calcutta, 1977, p. 9

political unrest, added pessimism to his anger. There is an element of desperation in the need to communicate it to the audience, to urge it to rise out of passiveness and apathy, to take up arms against a sea of troubles. He uses techniques of agit prop, with songs and ballet, satire and stylisation — addressing the audience directly. He wants involvement but he also urges action. The setting is Calcutta and the films are in Bengali. At the end of those four years he seemed spent. But only temporarily.

Sen came back to the struggle two years later in 1976 but went back in time and away from Calcutta in both setting and language, actual and cinematic, to make *Mrigayaa* (The Royal Hunt) in Hindi, in a tribal village, in pre-Independence days, in a narrative form. His essential attitude had not changed. The message of protest against exploitation continues. For *Oka Oorie Katha* (The Outsider) he transplanted Premchand's Hindi story *"Kafan"* from a village in the North to Andhra Pradesh in the South, and made it in Telugu. The anger here is transmuted by a fine alchemy into a timeless, magnificent allegory on poverty. In Govind Nihalani's *Aakrosh* made three years later, the young man in the isolation and helplessness of poverty, retreats into absolute silence. In Sen's *Oka Oorie Katha* the old father refuses to participate in his own victimisation and, with his son as his ally, he drops out. He rejects the codes and the canons of society. His demoniacal rage liberates him, frees him from conventional behaviour. He is not dehumanised by his poverty, he rises above it. The character is brilliantly created by Vasudeva Rao whom Mrinal Sen first saw in B.V. Karanth's *Chomanadudi*. Technique and content are fused in masterly fashion in this film. From *Bhuvan Shome* onwards, Mrinal Sen always worked with K.K. Mahajan, a Film Institute graduate, as his cameraman. Sen's own maturing assisted by the new technicians and actors entering the field, began with *Oka Oorie Katha*.

Parashuram (The Man with the Axe) 1978, was a mild anti-climax. Sen attempted to raise to a mythic dimension the story of a poor young migrant to the city where he discovers the poverty to be still more acute. *Parashuram* was like an interlude, for the following year he made *Ek Din Pratidin* (And Quiet Rolls the Day) and entered his most creative phase. He was done with experimentation. He had found himself. With *Ek Din Pratidin* (Literally and more appropriately: A Day Like Any Other) the bald statement gives way to the allusive detail, an effortless creation of atmosphere and a multi-layered density. Both *Oka Oorie Katha* and *Parashuram* dealt with concepts halfway between the real and the imagined. In *Ek Din Pratidin* the setting, the characters, the atmosphere are Bengali middle class. The awkward syntax and the restless camera are more controlled. The style of *Ek Din Pratidin*, as Sen says, developed organically. It is not an intellectual imposition arising from a desire to innovate. There is a unity of time and place, and chronological progression. One single night when the family waits in anxious irresolution for the daughter, the only wage earner of the family, who does not come home from her office. The lack of communication within the family, the anxiety for her physical safety becoming anxiety about what the neighbours will say; the vexation at the want of consideration in not informing them she will be late, the tension and the trauma, are palpable. Sen reveals the insecurity and fears of middle-class life and the claustrophobia of middle-class morality. The movements of the camera heighten the suffocating materialism of such an existence. The sound track is as carefully composed as the images. Underneath the actual events lie the peculiar, unresolved attitudes towards a working daughter who cannot be treated in the same manner as a working son. When she does return as dawn breaks, the relief is so great that no questions are asked. But in that long night, values have changed, necessity recognised. In that shifting of perspective lies the possibility of survival.

With *Akaler Sandhaney*, Sen returned to the theme of hunger, but viewed with the guilt of a middle-class conscience. In Mrinal Sen's film about making a film, a film crew descends on a village, there to recreate the conditions of the same 1943 Bengal famine that formed the core of

Baishey Shravana. The real and the imaginary come in brutal confrontation as the film crew realises that the life of Durga, the village girl, closely parallels the fictionalised Savitri in the film they are making. Reality breaks through the comfortably distant past, and the film makers appear as the exploiters. It is Mrinal Sen coming face to face with himself, and turning away guilt-stricken at what he sees.

Guilt, in fact, is the overriding emotion in these last films : guilt for affluence and plenty in the midst of want and squalor. But it is not overt, like the anger of the have-nots in the earlier films. It is the hidden, secret guilt of the haves, surfacing unexpectedly, breaking the pillars of complacency. In *Chaalchitra* (The Kaleidoscope) less assured than the two preceding films, it is a young man looking for a news story that will land him the newspaper job he covets. *Kharij* (The Case is Closed) ends the trilogy (why is it always a trilogy and not a 'quadrology'?) on the Calcutta middle class. The young couple with one small son, surviving with difficulty on the edge of respectability, is shattered by the death of the young servant boy they have employed. Not directly responsible for it, they come to realise their guilt in taking for granted the exploitation that the class they belong to has always practised.

By now Mrinal Sen has come closer to Satyajit Ray's humanism. He no longer assigns immediate responsibility to a class or a system, but tries to understand the anguish and uncertainty of the individuals who compose it. "In the state in which India finds itself," he said, "it is not sufficient to be a humanist."* Under Sen's new humanist concern, the Marxist still exists, less openly polemical, more profound, giving his cinema the capacity to alter perceptions at a more fundamental level than of immediate— and transient— communication!

Khandhar, (The Ruins) 1983, is again in Hindi. Sen was now a major national figure, and Hindi gave him an undoubtedly larger audience. Guilt in class relations is transferred to cowardice in a personal equation. There are more nuances, more shades of grey in this encounter between a young man from the city and the lonely young woman in the decaying feudal mansion in the countryside. She is the cousin of one of the friends in whose house the three young men spend a weekend away from the city (It is impossible not to see parallels in the themes if not the style of Ray and Sen, much closer than either might admit). Nothing is said, but the experience is deeply felt by both. He goes back to his frenetic life as a photographer. She remains, chained to her ailing mother's bedside. He is clearly disturbed by his cowardice but not enough to change. Reduced to a photograph on the wall of his studio, she is a constant reminder of the guilt he feels. She is profoundly altered by the brief contact, strengthened by the unfulfilled promise it held out momentarily, secure now in the conviction that beyond the torpor of her immediate circumstances, life exists, even for her.

---

* Interview in *Positif, op cit* p. 64

4

THE MIDDLE PATH

In countries where a new movement opposed to the popular cinema surfaced, it developed out of a compulsion felt by the filmmakers themselves to plumb the depths of their medium as a basic material with the richest potential for creative expression, as an art, or as an instrument of social change. In India it was the government that initiated the change, making it possible for a whole new generation to produce films which are often extremely critical of the government's functioning.

In 1957, at the Parliamentary discussions preceding the setting up of the Film Finance Corporation, suggestions were put forward which give clear indication of the prevailing state of the film industry and the attitude towards the cinema in general. Among the criteria to be adopted when sanctioning loans for films it was decided that the "human interest of the story," the "Indianness in theme and approach" and "characters with whom the audience can identify" must be of cardinal importance. It might appear that these would be the basic impulse behind any Indian film. But in its frenetic pursuit of entertainment and box office success the commercial cinema had moved so far away into a vague dream-territory that it bore no relation to anything.

In the early years the FFC was feeling its way, attempting a reform within the film industry itself, giving loans up to a fixed amount to established filmmakers regardless of the total cost of the finished film. Guarantees were demanded and commercial viability was a definite consideration. In fact, the Inter-Departmental Committee in its report in 1957 had advised that "loans should not be given to persons who had no previous experience as producers or directors." This was modified by the Board of Directors, when the FFC was created in 1960 to:

> "The Corporation (FFC) might also, in special cases, finance producers (*i.e. filmmakers*) who had not produced any picture in the past provided, looking to their technical and other qualifications, the Board of Directors was satisfied that the producer was likely to produce even as a first venture, a good quality film which would also be commercially successful."[*]

At this time the Film Institute had not yet been established, and the only newcomers with some technical expertise would necessarily be products of the film industry itself. However, the Corporation did give financial assistance to Satyajit Ray, Chetan Anand, V. Shantaram and

[*] Committee on Public Undertakings (1975-76): Seventy-Ninth Report, Film Finance Corporation Limited, New Delhi. Lok Sabha Secretariat March 1976, p. 16.

Bimal Roy, but also to others with entrenched positions in the heart of the commercial world. A few, like Mohan Segal, wished to make some kind of a departure, but they were too deeply imprisoned by the ideology that had conditioned them and the only style of filmmaking of which they had first-hand experience and knowledge. The Film Finance Corporation was swimming in unfamiliar waters in stressing "human interest", "Indianness", "identifiable characters in socially conscious stories." These were difficult to define, while concepts of style and form did not enter into the picture at all. In 1963, the FFC declined a loan to Ritwik Ghatak for *Aranyak,* a script he wrote based on a Bibhuti Bhushan Bandopadhyay story because Ghatak could not find a guarantor. Conflicting interests were built into the guidelines the FFC's Directors drew up. Socially conscious filmmakers were a rarity, "new" filmmakers had limited technical expertise, and only those who had already proved themselves financially viable could hope to find collateral security.

It was an impasse which lasted for some more years. Until 1975-76, social consciousness was being equated with "workers problems" and "village life", with the FFC claiming that it had financed some films that "depict village life" such as (Mrinal Sen's) *Bhuvan Shome* and (Mani Kaul's) *(Uski Roti)*! In the meantime, the norms for granting loans up to a certain amount without collateral security, had been modified. In 1964, under directions from Mrs. Gandhi,

Mrinal Sen's BHUVAN SHOME, 1969

then Minister for Information & Broadcasting, and under B.K. Karanjia's enlightened chairmanship, the Corporation took the decision to support newcomers wishing to make small-budget films, and that its objective should be to encourage "artistic" films, not merely "the usual type of films which may be a commercial success." The films of Satyajit Ray— *Charulata* in 1964, and *Goopy Gyne Baghe Byna* in 1968 — stand out among those supported at this time. In 1968 too, Mrinal Sen was granted a loan for *Bhuvan Shome* which was released in October 1969. It was to prove a landmark in that it was in Hindi and, despite its total dissimilarity with the normal Hindi film, it attracted a large enough audience not only to recoup its investment but to show some profit. It was the first clear indication that the market was ready for something different. Light, fresh, whimsical, it has the durable charm of a fairy tale.

In the year that *Bhuvan Shome* was released, the FFC granted loans to two other filmmakers making their first films, which started two distinct continuing trends — Basu Chatterjee for *Sara Akash* (The Whole Sky) and Mani Kaul for *Uski Roti* (A Day's Bread). Both, in radically different ways, broke with the established pattern. Basu Chatterjee was for many years a cartoonist with a leading, satirical journal. A film society regular, he was enchanted most of all by the comedies from Czechoslovakia and had long thought about making films himself. The FFC gave him the opportunity. In 1971, *Sara Akash* was released and found audiences as responsive as they had been to *Bhuvan Shome*. The low-budget, straightforward, coherent, mildly thought-provoking cinema was to become an established viable alternative to the

Mani Kaul's USKI ROTI, 1969

cinema of spectacle. Its style is neo-realistic, the content frequently social conflict, the structure linear narrative. It does not always come out on the side of radical change. Indian society, like its filmmakers, lives on too many levels at once for any statement to be totally unambiguous. There is protest, but there is also an implicit acceptance of the governing norms.

The realism in the work of many directors who emerged in the seventies, did cater to the demands of middle-class urban audiences, satiated with the entertainment provided by the (relatively) small number of Western, primarily American movies. In the early seventies, the import of Hollywood films was temporarily stopped as the government worked out terms more acceptable to India, of a new agreement with the American Motion Picture Export Association. Many of the Indian films that followed in the trail of *Sara Akash* were patterned on a fifties and sixties Hollywood model.

Sara Akash, made without stars, has the realistic setting of an extended middle-class family where the youngest, college-going son, is thrust by family pressure into an unwelcome marriage with a pretty, "educated" girl. The relationships within the family, the status of the brothers and their wives, of the daughters, married and unmarried, though treated with humour and a light touch, subscribe to established norms. Within its fold, the young man and his unjustly-blamed bride, discover each other in a customary development where love follows marriage. However, the sub-text betrays a number of conservative attitudes underlying the surface comedy. The young wife's education serves no useful purpose. It does not help her to cope with the situation in which she finds herself any better than her uneducated sisters-in-law. Her ability to read makes her the butt of jokes among the other women in the family. Arising from envy? Novels or magazines— all that she is ever seen reading— provide the young wife an escape from the taunts of her mother-in-law and the sulky silences of her husband. It is only his unhappy sister who sympathises with her. Abandoned by her own husband for another woman, she returns miserably to her father's home. Unwelcome, insecure, incapable of helping herself, she is a sharp contrast to the women in the real world who were beginning to work towards economic and social independence. She is obliged to go back to her husband who, having been discarded by the other woman, comes to claim her. Her mother pleads for her to be allowed to stay back but without any real hope or conviction, believing that the father is doing the socially correct thing in sending her back to what is well recognised as a life of misery. Significantly, none of the other younger women come to her aid. They too, are conditioned into believing that the woman's place is with her husband, whatever his faults.

In a later film, *Swami* (Lord & Master), 1977, Chatterjee returned to a somewhat similar theme, but with the roles reversed. The reluctant wife (Shabana Azmi), seeing the undemanding gentleness of her husband (Girish Karnad) and his mother's sarcasm is comparing him with his financially more successful brother, recognises his true worth. In this film too, the woman's obvious ability and character find an outlet only in anger or withdrawals into silence. Love and an understanding of each other, as in *Sara Akash*, flower after marriage.

The simplicity of *Sara Akash* was, however, a welcome contrast to the commercial cinema where even a similar plot would be drowned in songs, tears, dances and sentimentality. Its success with the audience started Chatterjee on a prolific career, private financing easily available. He began to specialise in light comedy, focussing on boy-meets-girl situations but wittily inverting the Hindi-film conventions. In a string of productions, he shows man-woman relations in contemporary, everyday settings in a funny, tender, ironic vein. But increasingly, Basu Chatterjee seemed in a hurry. The strokes became broader, heavier, the situations flimsier. The ability is apparent, dormant underneath the fluff, and he vindicated it in his latest film *Ek Ruka Hua Faisla*, 1985, a Hindi remake of *Twelve Angry Men*.

Between 1969 and 1973, the FFC gave loans to a number of small-budget (the term became synonymous with "non-commercial" therefore "different") films — to Basu Bhattacharya (Bimal Roy's one-time assistant) for *Anubhav* in Hindi, to Kantilal Rathod for *Kanku* in Gujarati, to

Chidananda Das Gupta for *Bilet Pherat* in Bengali, to Satyadev Dubey and Govind Nihalani for *Shantata, Court Chalu Ahe* in Marathi, to Shivendra Sinha for *Phir Bhi* and to Awtar Kaul for *27 Down*, both in Hindi.

With most of these, regardless of language, the "difference" lay principally in the subject and the straight-forward narrative style. Among the films he has made, Basu Bhattacharya's trilogy on the marital state which began with *Anubhav* (Experience) and continued with *Aavishkar* (Discovery) and *Grihapravesh* (The Housewarming) is noteworthy for the way he turns marriage into a love story. He is not stirred by that first fine careless rapture. "I don't consider that Laila and Majnu, or Romeo and Juliet, were in love. They were infatuated with each other and they died together. They did not live together," he says. Bhattacharya's films are about living together and what happens to men and women in such trying circumstances. Away from escapist dreams and social problems too large to handle, he enters into the lives of ordinary people coping with the most intimate details of daily living. Here, too, love succeeds marriage, but where most films end with that discovery, Bhattacharya's start with it and go on to examine the phase immediately following it. The Other — man or woman — in all three of these, remains an abstraction, operating as a catalyst, making the couple aware of what they had nearly lost. Although Bhattacharya's cinematic style hardly differs from what preceded it, the subject and the attitudes the films embody, are different enough to merit attention.

In *Kanku*, Kantilal Rathod goes about reversing the usual attitude towards widows in a subdued, naturalistic manner. From the rural milieu in Gujarat, he moved to love in a university setting in *Parinay* (Romance) in Hindi, with Shabana Azmi playing the young woman who follows her idealistic husband back to his village to set up a school. An interesting point is made through her mother who writes articles with Gandhian nobility about the infamy of class and caste differences. Her dilemma arises when she has to live up to those ideals in the face of her daughter's determination to marry beneath her class.

Shantata, Court Chalu Ahe (Silence! The Court is in Session) was Govind Nihalani's only venture into production and the first film he shot as an independent cameraman. Co-produced and directed by Satyadev Dubey, the writer who later worked on several of Shyam Benegal's scripts, it is based on a play by Vijay Tendulkar who also wrote the screenplay. A group of social workers in a village stage a mock trial as a pleasant diversion on a drowsy summer afternoon. The fun turns to tragedy as personal weaknesses, jealousies and resentments surface and the game becomes an inquisition, baring one woman's terrible secret. It was an early essay into what Tendulkar and Nihalani both were to develop in their later work.

The film society movement had been growing rapidly across the country. The first film society was founded in Bombay in 1943 by nine members interested only in seeing good films themselves. Their efforts were not directed towards spreading a love for cinema and creating a film culture. At Calcutta, on the contrary, the film society created in 1947 by Satyajit Ray, Chidananda Das Gupta, Hari Das Gupta and others, started a library of books and magazines, invited Renoir, Pudovkin and Cherkassov, Rossellini, John Huston, Frank Capra and others who happened to be in India, to address its members. They brought out a regular film bulletin, declaring in the opening issue in 1951: "the cinema in India has suffered from an almost complete lack of thought and sensibility and the film society movement is perhaps the only ground from which a new concept of Indian cinema can spring." The Calcutta film society, according to Chidananda Das Gupta, "established the idea that seeing good foreign films was essential for spreading disaffection with the low, imitative standard of Indian films. The important thing was to develop a genuine national cinema." Towards the end of the sixties, the Society raised the funds to produce a short documentary on Calcutta — *Portrait of a City*, which was directed by Chidananda Das Gupta. Mani Kaul saw this film, he says, when he was about fifteen, and it struck him that cinema had an exciting potential, even in India. "After that

I decided immediately that the thing to do was to direct a film. And I went off to the University library to read books on film."(*)

It took Chidananda Das Gupta several more years to take the decision to resign from his lucrative job with a business house in Calcutta and start making films himself. He was a member of the FFC's Board of Directors in 1969, and was one of the few who fought for a change in its policies. It was at this time that against great pressure from the established film industry the FFC gave Mrinal Sen the loan for *Bhuvan Shome*. Das Gupta resigned from the Board when he applied for financial assistance for his own film, *Bilet Pherat* (England Returned).

It was an ambitious first film composed of three separate segments connected by a single theme — the Indian who comes home from abroad and the radical adjustments he is required to make. Hilarious situations are underplayed to reveal a fine feeling for black comedy and an ironic, compassionate sense of humour that revels in absurdities. Soumitra Chatterjee, Anil Chatterjee, Nirmal Kumar and others are joined by Dasgupta's daughter Aparna Sen in the stories of three young men who return to Calcutta from Paris, Oxford and the United States.

It has minor flaws difficult to overcome in a first film with three separate stories, a cast that includes a stubborn donkey which, during the shooting, refused to bray, and a bull that refused to charge! The budget did not stretch sufficiently to allow Das Gupta's creativity full expression. Called "the only humorist in the Indian cinema" by a contemporary French critic, he could have developed a unique style of comedy, very different from the tone of Basu Chatterjee's. Das Gupta, however, soon afterwards abandoned film making to concentrate on writing.

Phir Bhi (All The Same) is perhaps the only film in the history of the Indian cinema whose entire focus is on a mother-daughter relationship. The grown-up daughter's excessive emotional dependence on the mother after the father's sudden death, the mother's maturity, her attempts to make her daughter face up to life and develop independence, are handled with delicate understanding. The mother is a University Professor, the daughter works as a telephone operator through which she has some contact with the callers without the need to establish real, living, demanding relationships. Afraid of life and emotional attachments, she lives a vicariously rich existence through conversations overheard on the telephone. The mother is a mature, attractive woman who is in love with a man we never see, but is prepared to sacrifice her own chance of happiness to help her daughter emerge out of her shell.

There are tentative signs of stylistic innovation which could have developed into an interesting style. But Shivendra Sinha has not yet made another film. *Phir Bhi* was made with a loan from the FFC, but in 1972 no commercial distributor was prepared to take it. A mother urging her daughter to meet other young people, to fall in love with a man of her choice; an older woman, a widow with an independent profession, in love and wanting to get married again — the subject and the style were probably too sophisticated and cut too deeply into the governing norms for general acceptability.

Uski Roti 1970, did not start a trend in the same way as *Sara Akash;* Mani Kaul's cinema is too personal and too unique to admit a following, but it did signal the arrival of a commitment to the cinema as a form of creative expression. *27 Down* (Banaras Express) showed some formal links with *Uski Roti,* made the year before Awtar Kaul started on his own film. An idealist in a materialistic world, a train ticket-inspector who had dreamt of being a painter, the young man (M.K. Raina) in the film is totally divorced from the life he is forced into. He is afraid enough of his domineering father to bow to his will, even to the extent of submitting to a marriage arranged for him, although he has fallen in love with a girl he meets on a train. With the last

(*) Interview in *Indian Cinema Superbazaar*, Vikas Publishing House, New Delhi, 1982, P230.

chance of an independent existence closed, he withdraws deeper into himself. A meeting with the girl kindles a small spark of hope which is quickly snuffed out. He drifts into nothingness. The train on which he travels endlessly becomes a metaphor for his life, going round in circles, leading nowhere. The girl Shalini (played by the star Raakhee) is also trapped in a life which has no exits, but she does not succumb to it. Coldly, firmly, she has the strength to carry on. The starkness is heightened by the photography in black and white by another Institute graduate, A.K. Bir, by the sparse sound track, the silences, the spaces through which the shrewish, insensitive rich wife's strident voice rings unpleasantly. Awtar Kaul was never able to develop his promising potential. He died accidentally soon after *27 Down* was completed.

Basu Chatterjee's SARA AKASH. 1969

5   SUBSTANCE AND STYLE

By the time Shyam Benegal made his first feature, *Ankur* (The Seedling) in 1974, the debate on the relative values and significance of form and content had begun. Mani Kaul's and Kumar Shahani's formalist concerns in *Uski Roti* (1971) and *Maya Darpan* (The Mirror of Illusion) a year later, were far removed from realist works about society and social relations.

  Ankur stayed within a naturalist tradition — humanism tinged with a strong ideological flavour in which caste differences, the exploitation of women and the underprivileged, were all under attack. It was to become Benegal's major theme: a society in which the bastions of inherited authority are under siege, as the traditionally exploited begin to assert the rights and privileges guaranteed under the Constitution. However, even within his own parameters there

Shyam Benegal's ANKUR, 1974

is a clash between form and ideology. In *Ankur,* the camera movements and cutting style are fluid, smooth, diluting the potential tension in the relations between the capitalist landlord (Anant Nag) and the class he represents, and the attractive young labourer's wife (Shabana Azmi) and the economic deprivation that she embodies. The colours are soft and pleasing, the lighting sharp and clear, indoors and out. But the linear narrative in itself was a departure from the pattern of the popular film, and Benegal's strength lay in strong stories and characterisations. In *Ankur,* the woman develops from a pretty but anonymous "labourer's wife" into an individual of marked character, subtly conveying a light, mocking recognition of her enforced subservience, as much as a knowledge that the landlord's power conceals an inherent lack of courage. His final act of brutality as he beats up her husband, is perfectly in keeping with a coward's panic-stricken outburst.

The actors were all beginners. Shabana Azmi and Sadhu Meher, the deaf-mute husband, had just graduated from the acting course at the Pune Film Institute, Anant Nag was a theatre actor from Bangalore working in Bombay. All were to become Shyam Benegal regulars, among the many more newcomers he discovered and introduced. Govind Nihalani was the cameraman who continued shooting Benegal's films until he turned to direction himself in 1980. *Ankur* was the first film for which Vanraj Bhatia composed the background music. For a first film, *Ankur* shows an impressive maturity, as remarkable in its own way as *Pather Panchali.*

The "new" cinema was just beginning in India, new modes of perception and technique for both film-makers and audience were still hazy and barely formulated. In the context of its time, *Ankur* was a major step. In the source of its financing lay the signs of a widening of the base of the means of production. With FFC-backed films winning recognition and prestige, private agencies entered the field. Blaze Advertising, for whom Shyam Benegal had made several commercials, was primarily a distribution company for advertising shorts. The two partners who had created it, proposed financing a feature film for him. He had carried around the script of *Ankur* for several years. Now, suddenly, it became possible to make it. It was the beginning of a long association between Benegal and Blaze.

Shyam Benegal's immediate critical and to some extent commercial success with *Ankur,* enabled him to make a film a year in addition to the documentaries and commercials he still produces. All his films are in Hindi, although *Kondura* (The Boon), 1977, was also made in Telugu as *Anugraham.* He moved in different directions with *Charandas Chor* (1975), *Bhumika* (The Role) 1977, *Junoon* (The Obsession) 1978, *Kalyug* (The Machine Age) 1981, and *Mandi* (The Market Place) 1984. The others — *Nishant* (Night's End) 1975, *Manthan* (The Churning) 1976, and *Arohan* (The Ascent) 1981, have many common elements. A rural setting, oppression, struggle, conflict, and resolution. Benegal wrote the script for *Ankur* himself with Satyadev Dubey writing the dialogue, but *Nishant* and *Manthan* had screenplays by Vijay Tendulkar. In all three, the conflict arises out of a situation created by the intrusion of an urban outsider. In *Ankur* it is the absentee landlord's son, isolated by his city ways and city clothes, his sense of unease and his solitariness heightened by the house in which he lives. The only concrete building in the village, it is a visible sign of power. In *Nishant,* it is the school teacher and his wife who bring unfamiliar values of democratic equality into an essentially feudal society; in *Manthan* a man from the city arrives in the village to organise a milk cooperative and disturb the feudal balance. But while *Ankur* has a slow, even rhythm and chooses the form of deliberate understatement to make its point, in the films that followed the action is more forceful, the anger more openly expressed. *Arohan* made some years later, with a script by Shama Zaidi, is his most overtly political statement. It was financed by the communist-led coalition government of the State of West Bengal which may or may not have influenced the mode of discourse Benegal chose. It traces a share-cropper's slow awakening to his constitutional rights, and his determined struggle to fight the endless battle of the poor and the landless against the entrenched power of the landlords. Adding to his difficulties are the repeated changes of the party in power in the State, which have repercussions on every level, increasing the difficulty of implementing laws. However, its strident tone, unusual for Benegal, make it into a straight-forward "message" film with little scope for nuances. As such it loses its impact. With everything seen in terms of black and white, oppressor against oppressed, its easy conclusions erode the intensity as well as the strong characterisations of Benegal's earlier films. There is an attempt at some formal innovation, but that does not advance beyond the opening credit sequence, and remains little more than a minor detail.

Between *Manthan* and *Arohan* were four films, each exploring a different area. *Charandas Chor,* 1975, made for the Childrens' Film Society, was based on a well-known folk story which Benegal adapted with Shama Zaidi. The theatre director Habib Tanvir also played a small role in it. In it, he introduced Smita Patil who would emerge as one of India's most intense actresses and remain a Benegal favourite. Benegal has said that he has never made a film on a subject he does not feel about "passionately, strongly". He is equally convinced that it is important for the cinema to "stop shadow boxing... it must get involved with contemporary situations... more films need to be made where you can be linked to your own time." In *Kondura/Anugraham* he ventures into another area, the hold of superstition. Although it has many Benegal characteristics — the interplay of power and sex in a non-urban setting, this time a fishing village, for which he returned to his own state of Andhra Pradesh, and its language Telugu — it does not carry conviction. In an attempt to communicate with local audiences, Benegal adopts many of the popular cinema's conventions. The young man who takes a vow of celibacy so that a boon granted him may be effective, does not tell his wife the reason for his abstinence. It is a typical Hindi-cinema device where misunderstandings grow through a lack of communication for which there is no apparent justification. The images of Smita Patil in the young man's erotic fantasies approximate so closely to the commercial cinema that they seem to legitimise it. The highly expressive acting and naturalist style do little to support the intended purpose of protest and criticism.

With *Bhumika,* Benegal entered the urban world for the first time. Based on the life of the actress Hansa Wadkar, a flamboyant star of the Marathi stage and cinema in the thirties, the period setting gives Benegal an opportunity to show glimpses of the films of the times, the manner in which they were made, the people behind the scenes as also social attitudes towards the movies and the stars. Benegal has said that for him it is important to construct the milieu through which the individual emerges more clearly. In *Bhumika,* the care given to the milieu through a period which covers the life of the actress (played by Smita Patil) from childhood, showing the early stages of the emergence of a middle class, is less evident in the construction of the character herself. Her individuality, her courage, her disregard for conventions, are quickly established. From then on there is little further development of the character. Her eventful life, her varied experiences, her many love affairs, with the shadowy presence of her husband hovering over them, are never internalized. Only at the end, when her daughter tells her she is pregnant without first informing her that she is married, does one see that, despite the unconventional life she has lived, the conditioning has been so strong that she reacts with orthodox distress. It is a revealing moment. Though there is a weakness in the structure, with its many flashbacks and an overlong introductory section dealing with the actress' childhood, Benegal's command over the handling of crowds, in building up scenes of tension, in capturing moments of intensity, is admirable.

Junoon and *Kalyug* confirmed his technical control. *Junoon* had the historical background of the first Indian uprising against British rule in 1857. The oppression of caste and class made way for the oppression of one country by another in a film conceived on a scale as grand as its subject. Girish Karnad and Benegal collaborated on the screenplay, based literally on the epic

Mahabharata where the feud between two branches of the same family lead to the great battle of Kurukshetra. In *Kalyug,* the characters from the Mahabharata are easily identifiable as the business rivalry between the cousins ends in the destruction of both. A large cast, complicated relationships, oblique references to corruption in high places, all the ills of today's world. Both these films were produced by the popular star Shashi Kapoor who also acts in them. Shyam Benegal seemed to have opted for a kind of cinema easily accessible to large audiences, serious, essentially simple, straightforward narrative in the classic Hollywood style.

Benegal, whose first cousin was Guru Dutt, had grown up in Hyderabad seeing the Hollywood films commercially released in the theatres. He expanded his horizons of cinema when he moved to Bombay and began seeing European films. But the major influence in his work remains Hollywood. In his next film *Mandi* the text gets slightly blurred. On the surface a comedy set in a small-town brothel, it never really works. Prostitution, especially today, is hardly the stuff of comedy, and the falsely sentimental atmosphere at the brothel with the girls living in companionable harmony with the motherly madame (brilliantly portrayed by Shabana Azmi), is more ridiculous than amusing. Elements of strangeness and tragedy are added through the characters of two other young women. With the one (Smita Patil) treated like a cherished daughter, the madame has a peculiar relationship compounded of protectiveness and lesbian undertones. The other, (Srila Mazumdar) sold into prostitution, is the dark side of the comedy. With her attempted suicide, bitterness intrudes into the make-believe world. Incidental characters rarely rise above the level of cliches — most obvious is the stern spinsterish social worker who comes to visit the brothel. None of the elements are integrated into a well-structured whole, surprisingly for Benegal whose earlier work was marked by well-knit stories and a sensitive concern for women. From *Mandi* he moved into a totally new world with *Trikal* (Past, Present and Future), 1985. A period setting. Goa. The Portuguese domination is about to end, the Indian army waiting to move in. But these momentous historical movements are perceived only faintly in the background and seem incidental to the central family drama. As with many other Benegal films the milieu and the ambience are lovingly recreated, aided considerably in this instance by Nitish Roy's art direction. The soft, glowing interiors filmed mostly by candle-light, muted sounds and languorous movements evoke a past that knows it has no future. Visual pleasure takes precedence over structure, even the drama surrounding the young nationalist, a fugitive from the stern arm of Portuguese law, is de-dramatised until its significance fades. The film raises many questions, touches on several issues and shies away from them.

In a hectic working life of 11 years Benegal has made 12 feature films, two feature-length documentaries — one as a co-production with the Soviet Union on Prime Minister Nehru, one on Satyajit Ray — plus around 600 commercials and 30 documentaries. That is hardly a schedule that leaves much time for introspection or careful planning.

Bhuvan Shome, Sara Akash and *Ankur* proved that audiences were prepared for films that demanded something more from them than the passive response expected by the consumerist cinema. But the films in this genre, as much as the intellectually demanding work of a body of mostly Film Institute trained directors, were few and far between. In 1974, M.S. Sathyu made *Garam Hawa* (Hot Wind). With many years in the theatre and strongly influenced by his association with the Indian Peoples' Theatre Association, he took up a theme no Hindi film had attempted in all these years — the tragic impact of the partition of India on the lives of ordinary people. In *Garam Hawa* an average middle-class Muslim family refuses to leave its home in Agra to migrate to the newly created state of Pakistan — an emigration that had been forced on millions on both sides of the border. As one by one relatives and friends make the move, the isolation of the family grows. An economic slide results from rapidly escalating change. An awareness of communal tension is felt, if not actually identified, but fundamentally decent human values survive. A crisis is reached, and resolved, as the decision to leave is renounced at the last moment when the youngest son jumps out of the horse-carriage carrying the family to the railway station (and on to Pakistan) to join a procession of striking workers. The father follows him, his choice made. Nationalism wins out over narrower considerations of community and religion. Playing the main role of the father was Balraj Sahni. A very successful star of the Bombay Hindi film (he also played the lead in *Dharti Ke Lal, Do Bigha Zameen, Anuradha*), Balraj Sahni had been a member of the Indian Peoples' Theatre Association in the forties. *Garam Hawa* was based on a story by Ismat Chugtai, the screenplay is by Sathyu's wife Shama Zaidi — later Shyam Benegal's collaborator on the scripts of several films, the dialogue by Kaifi Azmi, the celebrated poet, lyric writer, and last but not least, Shabana Azmi's father. With such an array of talent behind him, with a mixed cast of professional actors and newcomers, Sathyu produced a film memorable for its delicate handling of a potentially volatile political issue. Hindu-Muslim relations had been punctuated by periodic flare-ups in the years after the country was divided. The Censor Board was nervous that feelings could be exacerbated by a film on this subject, and the commercial cinema, afraid of the Censor Board's possible reaction, had left it severely alone. Sathyu's film, for which he received a loan from the Film Finance Corporation after it had approved the script, moved beyond the narrow, political dimension to the larger tragedy of all those turned into refugees by events over which they have no control. However, the Censor Board refused to pass it. Sathyu had to appeal to higher powers in Delhi where it was eventually cleared by Prime Minister Indira Gandhi herself. Far from inciting inter-communal clashes, it proved deeply moving to large audiences and played to full houses all over the country. In 1975, it received the award for the best film on national integration.

In none of the four films he has made since then has Sathyu recaptured the moral anguish of *Garam Hawa.* For the next film, he returned from Bombay and Hindi to his home state of Karnataka and made *Kanneshwara Rama* (The Legendary Outlaw), 1977, followed by *Chitegu Chinte* (The Restless Corpse), 1979, in Kannada. One reason was the subsidy being offered by the State Film Development Corporation, another, very likely one, was the growing regionalism, with many young directors returning "home" in search of roots, asserting a regional identity to counter the rootlessness of the popular film. Film Development Corporations were being set up in most States, offering incentives to filmmakers. The result was an infrastructure of studios and laboratories, and a surge in film-making in regional languages. Since the highly inflated Entertainment Tax is collected by State Governments, it was an initiative that paid dividends in plenty while helping directors to make their first films, much as the NFDC was doing at the national level. With *Kanneshwara Rama,* Sathyu flirted with "commercialism" in the story of a bandit, a latter-day Robin Hood; with *Chitegu Chinte* he attempted something very unusual in India: political satire. The idea was fascinating, but the handling was maladroit. Both met with indifferent reactions. Sathyu had directed these two films for two different producers and chafed under the restrictiveness of the situation. In 1980 he took a loan from the NFDC to become his own producer. He turned to what was becoming his major preoccupation — political themes presented in a realistic manner. He first made *Bara* (The Famine) still in Kannada, remaking it in Hindi as *Sookha* (Drought). A small town, a dedicated Government official, corruption and cynicism at the political level where the fires of inter-communal tension are deliberately kindled for immediate political gain, are the core. Sathyu had opted for the cinema as a tool of social transformation. But the message is patent, the characterisation sketchy, the grace and warmth of *Garam Hawa* missing. Although the end is not defeatist and Sathyu stresses the strength of the individual, the film is never able to transcend its immediacy.

In *Kahan Kahan Se Guzar Gaya* in Hindi, 1985, for which Sathyu received a grant from the West Bengal State Government, the arena of the ideological struggle is the upper middle-class youth of Calcutta. Rebelling against the affluence and complacency of their parents they turn to radical political movements much as the sons of the bourgeois industrialist class in an earlier era, in another context, had expressed their protest by becoming Bohemian artists. Drifting through a variety of experiences in search of significance, the spoilt and unhappy scion of one such family, goes from self-forgetfulness in the arms of his successful singer girl-friend to active participation in a Marxist group led by her stern brother. The confusion of the Left movement forms the background to the confusion in the young man's life where ideas, values, systems, relationships are uncertain and appear meaningless. But where *Bara/Sookha* ended on a note of hope, *Kahan Kahan...* offers none because, Sathyu believes, a positive ending would have been unrealistic and, therefore, propagandist. The pessimism is realistic, no doubt, but the faithful reproduction of reality serves only to reconfirm it. Sathyu is seeking strong reactions from the young. If they can be stirred into anger, passion, argument, he will be satisfied. Looking back on *Garam Hawa,* he finds it too emotional and sentimental: "the issues we face in the country today are too important", he insists, and feels the need to provoke people into awareness if not action through his films.

In the ten years that separate *Kahan Kahan Se Guzar Gaya* from *Garam Hawa,* the world had changed considerably. The sense of security represented by Government institutions had been replaced by an erosion of faith in its functioning and machinery.

In the seventies conditions within the country had begun to show visible signs of change. In 1964, an era had ended with the death of Nehru. From a sense of pride, of political and social stability, the fall was sudden, with the nadir coming at the end of the decade. The death of two Prime Ministers in quick succession (Shastri died in 1966) was mitigated by victory in the 1965 war with Pakistan. This, in turn, was overshadowed by the food crisis following periods of severe drought in 1965 and 1967. Dependence for food on outside aid cast a long shadow on

M.S. Sathyu's KAHAN KAHAN SE GUZAR GAYA. 1985

national self-confidence. The seventies started in introspective questioning and doubt. It was the beginning of a period of political instability when the Party at the Centre found itself out of power in Kerala in the South and in the entire Northern belt from the Punjab to West Bengal. The effect of the Green Revolution which ended the food shortage dramatically, was evident by 1974 and restored a degree of self-assurance. India had survived war and drought and seen two peaceful changes of power at the Centre. But both the spreading democratic process and the Green Revolution had wrought other changes which would have unforeseen repercussions. In the fifties and through to the sixties, political power was vested in people who had for the most part a sound legal training. Their roots may have been rural but their education was urban and Western. Adult suffrage and the widening democratic practice brought into the system people representing rural areas who were not steeped in what is basically an alien value system. One man one vote, equality before the law, the administrators and the police as arbiters and upholders of the law, were concepts foreign to the Indian ethos. Accustomed to a feudal hierarchy where some are more equal than others, and where an individual's loyalty and responsibility is to his family and his community in that order, concepts of merit, fair play and impartial justice were difficult to grasp. This cultural contradiction began to invade the urban centres and reached a climax in the early seventies. In the agricultural belt, the Green Revolution strengthened the hands of those who already enjoyed positions of privilege. They had the influence, they had the money, and as demands of production grew and were met, the more political power this class was able to garner. Conditions became critical towards the mid-seventies.

Drought in parts of the country in 1973-74 was contained by the Green Revolution, but in October 1973 oil prices quadrupled as a result of the world oil crisis. Corruption spread and so did the peoples' anger. Mounting disaffection came to a head in the Navnirman agitation in Gujarat over the acute shortage of cooking oil. The moral authority of the Congress Party was being eroded. In the Gujarat Assembly, although it commanded a two-third majority, the Congress Government had to be dismissed, and the Assembly dissolved. The agitation that brought it to its knees spread to Bihar where its leadership was assumed by Jayaprakash Narayan. As bitter divisiveness increased, the Allahabad High Court judgement unseating the Prime Minister on a flimsy technicality aggravated the crisis in the Indian political system. A state of emergency was declared in June 1975 and lasted for two years until elections were held in March 1977, restoring a firm commitment to democracy, a commitment strengthened by the brush with authoritarianism so discordant with the ideals and aspirations with which modern India had fought for independence. The embitterment with public life it had created found angry expression at the end of the Emergency in countless magazines and journals which sprang up after 1977.

And in the cinema.

The mood of the country had altered beyond recognition. In Bombay, home of the film industry, the enforcement of prohibition in the fifties was one of the main causes of the rise of an underworld; smuggling, prostitution, an increasing crime rate and the emergence of a lumpen element that was to take over virtual, if invisible control of the city. In the early seventies, the commercial cinema began to express these conditions explicitly. Violence and sex, rape, vendetta, denigration of the legitimate forces of law and order, a vaunting and flaunting of villainy, corruption and illegally acquired wealth, reflected the disenchantment with established institutions. Honesty was seen as the virtue of fools, the individual outside the pale of the social order emerged as the hero. The shape of the popular cinema was transformed. But in an extraordinary sleight-of-hand, the undercurrent remained feudal, traditional and conservative as this same cinema upheld family ties, the veneration of the mother, an entire hierarchical social order. The only difference was that in the new order "to protect one's sister was to rape someone else's."*

By the end of the seventies, another genre of cinema had emergd somewhere between the commercial and the "new". It tackled such issues head-on, with no juggling of contradictions, revealing them as such, portraying the decay of urban and rural life in starkly realistic terms.

When Govind Nihalani decided to direct his own feature film, he discussed script ideas with the playwright Vijay Tendulkar who had written *Shantata Court Chalu Ahe,* plus Benegal's *Manthan* and *Nishant.* Tendulkar at the time was using his Nehru fellowship to study "The Emerging Patterns of Violence in Contemporary Society". Out of their discussions came the script for Nihalani's first film, *Aakrosh* (The Cry of the Wounded) in 1980. Although the situation is not unfamiliar, the assumption of privilege and therefore exploitation, it is lifted on to a more contemporary plane. The expanded cast of characters, the intensity of the gaze to which their motivations and actions are subjected, gives it a raw power.

Satyajit Ray had found universal human truths in rural India. To Ray's humanist vision, Shyam Benegal brought a criticism of social practice, giving his films a specific historical location. Nihalani added a political-contemporary connotation, showing the contradictions and distortions that emerge as feudalism passes painfully into democracy. Govind Nihalani's picture of the rural milieu is stark, non-sentimental, contemporary. Gone is the eternal India of the past, submissively bending its head before a centuries-old feudal hierarchy. Nihalani's landlord is not the cliche of the familiar screen money-lender. He is in alliance with the local officials, politicians and police in a new and much more threatening power combine. The

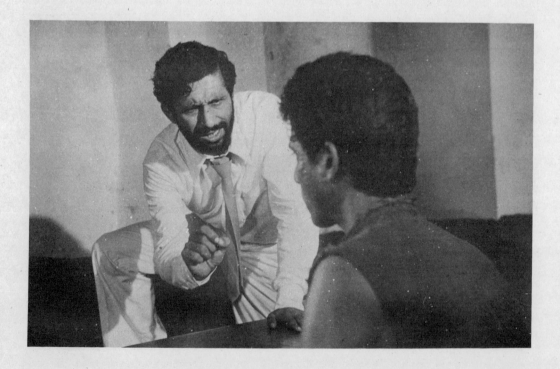

Govind Nihalani's AAKROSH. 1980

* Kumar Shahani, "Politics & Ideology" in *Indian Cinema, Superbazaar, op cit, p 73.*

metaphor of the voicelessness of the helpless is translated into a literal refusal to speak by the young tribal (Om Puri) in *Aakrosh*. He is accused of murdering the wife he loved by the very people who raped and then killed her. He is tried for the crime, and finally convicted. The scene when he runs round and round the house, from within whose impenetrable walls he can hear his wife's cries, the anguish of helplessness rising within him, is a moment of rare intensity. How can justice be rendered when it is not a single individual but society itself, embodied by the doctor, the policemen, the politician, and the businessman, which is corrupt and rotten? But it is the individuals determined to fight on, despite the odds, who signify the persistence and the survival of hope.

That underlying current of hope is put severely to the test in his later film *Ardh Satya* (Half Truth), 1983. Power, in this film is so absolute that it corrupts anyone within its circle who tries to break it. The naive young lawyer (Naseeruddin Shah) of *Aqkrosh* is replaced by the novitiate policeman with idealism shining bright in his eyes (Om Puri) in *Ardh Satya;* the cynical older lawyer of the former film (Amrish Puri) by the worldly-wise older policeman of the latter (Shafi Inamdar). Both are pragmatists who have come to terms with their social and political environment, and recognise the limits within which they can survive. Both try and make the younger ones understand the forces ranged against them. But while the lawyer is aroused by this understanding to oppose them, the policeman in the later film succumbs. Terror belongs to both films, but the psychological explanation offered in *Ardh Satya* is too inadequate to be satisfying. The condemnation of corruption and violence becomes an acceptance of both in an internal splintering of the text. The few years that separate the two films show the extent to which the lumpen have taken hold of our lives and our imagination.

In both films, the woman's (Smita Patil) role is peripheral. The conflict is between the men. But her brief appearance as the wife in *Aakrosh* is electrifying, and the memory of it permeates the entire film. In *Ardh Satya,* the role is sketchy to the point of meaninglessness. Representing the forces of decency, she remains a symbol, never becoming an individual.

Between the two films, Govind Nihalani made *Vijeta* (The Victory) 1982, a sentimental portrait of a family with an Air Force pilot son. The success of *Ardh Satya* had made him a commercially attractive director in great demand. Shashi Kapoor produced Nihalani's *Vijeta*. He played the father, his son Kunal the pilot son and Rekha, the reigning star of the times, the mother. With this star cast, Nihalani produced a "clean commercial" with patriotic underpinnings, notable for its spectacular aerial photography which he did himself. Around the same time he worked on Richard Attenborough's *Gandhi,* as the second-unit director-cameraman.

With his fourth film, Nihalani moved into another area altogether. *Party* 1984, works as an investigation into Bombay's intellectual elite, closeted in its own small world, alienated alike from its affluent peers and the active revolutionaries with whom it would like to ally itself, uneasy, disturbed, a prey to neurosis and alcohol. With a cast drawn principally from the theatre and written by another Marathi playwright, Mahesh Elkunchwar, its treatment is closer to the theatre than Nihalani's other films. The closed, claustrophobic world the characters inhabit is captured physically and psychologically through the house where the party takes place. All the inner contradictions they hide under the sheen of sophisticated argument are revealed through the long evening.

Perhaps Nihalani himself felt not quite comfortable with a single setting and limited characters, because other extraneous incidents and characters are introduced which only distract from the central, absorbing core of the theme. At the very end he uses the same shock tactics — an act of terrible violence — with which *Aakrosh* and *Ardh Satya* close. But the physical expression of violence in those films is out of place in the literary mode of *Party,* where the last scene seems an arbitrary imposition, upsetting the tone of what precedes it.

Govind Nihalani's images of graphic violence, the caressing treatment of it by the camera and his own technical skill, make for a highly dramatic style. In *Party* he seemed to be working towards a more reflective cinema. But under the effect of the terrible final image the consciousness sought to be raised through the self-questioning, the moral confusion, the personal traumas — which touch on fundamental issues — all recede into the background. The shock tactics make for a basically affective cinema, ideal for highly emotional, highly volatile audiences in India.

With *Aghaat* (Blood of Brothers), 1985, Nihalani reverts to the theme of political/ideological conflict and simmering violence. The ideology of the Marxist trade union working towards change through a politicisation of the workers is seen as ineffectual against the violence easily used by the politically ambitious leaders of the other, upstart union with no commitment to anything but themselves. The role of exploiter thus passes, clearly unintentionally, from the Management to the Union. The dialogue between the distressed Marxist leader (Om Puri) and the Party ideologue at the scene of the violent confrontation they have engineered, echoes the debate between Krishna and Arjuna on the battlefield of Kurukshetra in the Mahabharata. A strange mix indeed of Marxism and the Gita! The victory of the Marxist union with which the film closes can only be a temporary triumph so filled is it with self-contradictions.

Nihalani has a curious talent for creating memorable villains who overpower the film. Perhaps the presence of unsavoury characters in our midst has been so thoroughly internalized that they naturally dominate their environment. Sadashiv Amrapurkar did it in *Ardh Satya*. Gopi in *Aghaat* (only his second role in a Hindi film; he first appeared in Mani Kaul's *Satah Se Uthata Admi*) is a magnetic, menacing presence.

The links that were being forged in the cinema at this time reflect the growing integration in society itself, which was becoming more mobile and flexible. In the cinema, it brought together people from widely disparate backgrounds, language, education and upbringing. Govind Nihalani's family had been forced to emigrate from Sind (now in Pakistan) at the partition of India. They settled in Udaipur where Govind grew up, permitted by his orthodox family to see only mythological films. The fascination with special effects made him determined to enter the field of cinematography. It was an interest strongly opposed by his father until the family priest announced that it was indicated in his horoscope. The inevitable was gracefully accepted. The first book on film Nihalani ever read was Eisenstein's "Notes of a Film Director". From mythologicals and an education primarily in Sanskrit, the move into the rarified world of Bombay's elite is not as long a journey as it might seem on the surface: it is part of the social transformation taking place.

Yet Nihalani continues to make repeated references to mythological figures — much as the commercial cinema does. But, says Nihalani, "unlike the commercial cinema which uses mythological references to support the status quo which they promote, we refer to mythology to support an action for change."

In this explicit desire to support "action for change", "communication" becomes the guiding principle, much as "entertainment" is for the frankly commercial school. Little attention is paid to form. This preoccupation with content has misled some into equating realism with "serious cinema" — "good" films that do not estrange audiences. Realism is identified with images of misery and exploitation in the villages. And in the cities: political malfunctioning, the callousness of the privileged, the wretchedness of those living at the edge of poverty in the shadow of luxury skyscrapers. What it reveals most directly is the rise of the lumpen in the cities without questioning it. The filmmakers paint a grim, cheerless picture rarely redeemed by a touch of humanity or of art.

The aim of finding a language with which to communicate with audiences by the commercial cinema, not to be "too avant-garde and esoteric" makes, with some exceptions, for a statement so clear-cut that there is little complexity left in either the situations or in the characters. Nor is there any real desire to extend the medium of cinema, to understand its capacity to go beyond immediate communication into a deeper level of perception. This simple communicative cinema reflects the turmoil, the anxiety, the anger, of contemporary conditions without quickening the imagination. The conclusion is predictable. The environment is what it is. One knows it, recognises it. No new consciousness is raised through a mirror image of it. Occasionally, a single scene or a performance or an unexpected insight, lights up the screen. In *Chakra* (Vicious Circle), 1980, made by Rabindra Dharmaraj (a young advertising executive, he died shortly after completing this first film), Smita Patil's notorious bathing scene in the urban slum does more than titillate the audience, although it was used for that express purpose in the publicity campaigns of the film. It underlines the dehumanising quality of poverty where one's most private acts have to be performed in the public gaze.

As social realism became the unfortunate order of the day, more and more filmmakers turned to it, winning national awards and acclaim along the way. In 1983, another Film Institute graduate, Prakash Jha, made an innocuously pleasant film *Hip Hip Hurray*. Set in a college, it extols the good, old-fashioned virtues of sportsmanship and fair play. The simple approach, the story itself, is reminiscent of Hollywood in its prime. It points out the strength and rewards of such qualities through an appeal to the basic decencies. But for his next film which, in point of fact, he had wanted to do first, Jha moved into the heart of rural India, to his home state of Bihar, to expose the appalling practice of *Panha* — the manner in which landlords acquire bonded labour by implicating ignorant and naive young men in crimes and then offering them shelter and protection from the law in return for life-long bondage. The character of the landlord and the oppression of the Harijan workers is unchanged since the cinema first showed the stirrings of a social conscience back in the silent era but the methods and means have been streamlined. The harassment of the Harijans at the time of national elections, the image of the uncaring politicians and of a callous press, give it a contemporary flavour. The picture of the downtrodden workers is bleak in the extreme. Protest, far from being a possibility, is ruled out altogether.

Prakash Jha's personal commitment to exposing and condemning this system cannot be questioned. But putting it across in a film is another matter altogether. In *Damul,* the beauty of the images and the lyricism of the camera movements create a soft, romantic mood at variance with the immanent violence of the situation. It is not clear where Prakash Jha stands. Does he identify with the Third Cinema, defined as one which "seeks to decolonize minds and lead to a transformation of society?" If so, *Damul* does not succeed. The reality Jha presents is no doubt exactly and faithfully reproduced but, as Alexander Kluge says, "the motive for realism is never confirmation of reality but protest." Realism in *Damul* has little impact beyond shock or pity. Protest dissolves into catharsis in the culminating individual act of revenge. Jha has not tried to develop a film language as ideologically determined as the content. When horror is clothed in beauty, the text splinters. What results is not "a politicization of cinema but an aestheticization of ideology."*

Greed for power, or money; the politician as villain; violence that hangs over the lives of ordinary, decent people trying to live according to values of probity and integrity; these were becoming the recognizable traits of the new cinema. Ramesh Sharma, in his first feature *New Delhi Times,* 1985 has given it a slightly different twist. From persecution in the villages where most of these films are set, he takes us into the midst of the influential, urban elite and reveals how thin is the shell into which we withdraw, assuming that our privileged position immunises us from the terror that stalks others less sheltered than we are. As such, it is an important film,

---

* Teshome H. Gabriel "Third Cinema in the Third World: The Aesthetics of Liberation", UMI Research Press, Ann Arbor, Michigan.

exposing the myth of security in affluence as a myth, forcing us out of our complacency, making us see that in going along with the decay in the ethical and social order, we are as vulnerable as those more helplessly exposed to it. It brings the fear and the violence home to us and lays the blame squarely on those who become a part of it through the refusal to protest.

New Delhi Times is designed as a political thriller with a journalist as the principal protagonist. It says as much about the disintegration of values and political malfeasance as it does about the impulse that drives a journalist to pursue a story and expose wrongdoing, regardless of the personal danger he courts through his persistence. Sharma does not succumb to the obviousness of making the journalist a young reporter full of zeal and enthusiasm, clashing with older, wiser, more cynical heads. Instead, Shashi Kapoor plays the mature, senior, editorial level journalist, happily married to a woman (Sharmila Tagore) who has a demanding profession of her own as a lawyer. It is an equal relationship between two warm, loving individuals. In their own different ways, through the exercise of their professions, they are not unaware of the ugliness of the world around them. But they fight their cases, write their stories, from the safety and comfort of their insulated surroundings. Until the ugliness they are fighting against enters their own lives and the tension builds to a suspense-laden climax. It is a clever combination of serious content and effective story-telling although a closer look reveals certain anomalies in the construction of character and plot. One wishes also that a little more of the lawyer wife at work had been shown. It was an ideal occasion to break definitively with the

Ramesh Sharma's NEW DELHI TIMES. 1985

traditional mould and show the woman as a rational, capable individual. Sharma only hints at it.

It is beautifully shot by Subroto Mitra. Fluid camera movements and invisible editing change suddenly to jerky handheld shots and quick cutting as riots explode in a small town. Muffled sounds and jazz on the sound track help in creating a tense atmosphere and give the film a polished Hollywood finish.

Since the seventies positions and crises had been emerging at all points, for filmmakers as much as for audiences and critics. Praise for the realistic genre, the wide acceptability of a "middle" cinema was proving a setback to those attempting imaginative innovation or simply exploring the medium in different ways.

Jabbar Patel attempted it, and quickly retreated. His first film *Samna* (The Confrontation), 1975, based on an original script by Vijay Tendulkar, is the story of a conflict between a village politician and an impoverished school teacher who threatens to expose his crooked ways. Patel's theatre background showed through in the staginess of *Samna,* but in *Jait re Jait* (The Victory) 1977, he uses techniques acquired in directing plays, to interesting effect. For this film, he worked out a musical form using the folk songs and dances of Maharashtra in a story that questions traditional beliefs, myths, the stuff of reality, particularly in tribal, rural India. They are exploded as mere superstition in this tale of a joyful, virtuous young drummer (Mohan Agashe) in love with a divorced girl from his tribe (Smita Patil). The anger that succeeds his loss of faith in the tribal god ends in tragedy, his actions leading to the girl's accidental death. The script is by another Marathi playwright, Satish Alekar, but Patel gave it an innovative, musical structure. However, *Jait re Jait* suffered the same fate as other "experimental" films: audiences were not ready for it, and Patel abandoned this form for conventional narrative in his subsequent films, satisfying himself with injecting a political message into them. *Simhasan* (The Throne) is a satirical exposure of political practices. With three films in Marathi, with audiences and attention thus limited to a single region, Patel followed *Umbartha* (Threshold) 1982 with a Hindi version of it the next year as *Subah* (Morning).

In yet another Tendulkar script, the film poses the questions which urban, wealthy, highly educated young women are asking themselves today. It shows a woman's search for relevance, for herself as an individual human being, her sense of emptiness even when accompanied by affluence and an understanding husband (Girish Karnad). Whether to stay within the heart of the very modern joint family where the childless brother-in-law and wife dote upon her little daughter, to work with the dynamic mother-in-law, to accept the conveniences and privileges her comfortable circumstances offer, or to strike out on her own, to use her education in the way she thinks would have some use, and prove, for her, the most satisfying? She opts for the latter. Scattering norms to the winds, the film never suggests that the woman has no call to be dissatisfied when she is a wife and mother, nor even to hint that her sense of dissatisfaction might stem from not having a son, so long held up as the final fulfilment of a woman's biological and social *raison d'etre*. With her husband's reluctant concurrence, she accepts a two-year assignment as Director of a Centre for Deserted Women in a neighbouring town. Exterior to her personal evolution but largely responsible for it are the women she comes across at the Centre. For the first time in her life she is brought face to face with the real difficulties women face: desertion and rape, with prostitution as the only answer to extreme poverty, attempted suicide and lesbianism. It is a corrosive exposure of the pompousness, hypocrisy and selfishness of those who run such "homes", who treat women as objects without questioning the forces that reduce them to this abject state. Totally caught up in her work and the women she is responsible for, she grows in stature herself. Her husband comes unexpectedly to visit her and finds her preoccupied and distraught. Eventually forced into resigning by the governing body of the Centre, she returns home, not defeated but determined to continue the battle. She finds her daughter emotionally bound to her aunt and uncle. The husband has become involved with another woman. He tells her he will break off the relationship but that it will take time. Her reaction to the disclosure is stronger than we have been led to expect from earlier behaviour. The film ends with her taking a train to an unidentified destination, starting a metaphorical journey into life, a smile playing about her lips.

There are ambivalences in the film. No attempt is made, for instance, to examine the relationship between the husband and wife or the mother and daughter. Her restlessness has no apparent cause, leading some to interpret her as basically neurotic. The weakness is in the script, which skims over details in projecting an over-all idea. Nevertheless, it offers powerful support to the woman's right to choose the way she wants to live, responding to a need audiences are beginning to feel for ideas that break the mould of thought frozen for centuries.

Jabbar Patel's—UMBARTHA. 1982

Jabbar Patel still divides his time between theatre and film. His stage production of *Ghasiram Kotwal* as a musical has become a classic. He effectively adapted (in Marathi) Brecht's *Threepenny Opera* to Indian situations, with Indian music, and has long planned to make a film of it in Hindi.

A doctor by profession, Jabbar Patel commutes to Pune from his rural hospital fifty miles away for all-night rehearsals with his theatre group. The hospital, which he runs with his doctor wife, keeps him in close touch with the enormity of the difficulties most rural people face in India. The plight of women is particularly acute.

Maharashtra, with Pune — more than its capital Bombay — as its cultural and intellectual centre, has all along been in the forefront of social reform and political action. It was here that Bal Gangadhar Tilak in pre-Independence days launched his magazine *Kesari* with the famous cry, "Freedom is my birthright and I shall have it." He was followed by the great social reformers Dr. Ambedkar and Maharshi Karve, propagating revolutionary ideas of rights for women and equality of castes.

The social reform movement became established in Maharashtra ahead of other States with the demand for education for all traditionally suppressed groups, women on the whole, men and women both from the "backward classes". A deeply embedded social structure, though, is not so easily displaced. Neither did job opportunities open up instantly. When Dr. Ambedkar's Republican Party split up in the sixties, angry young men were denied a political outlet. A movement against the landed aristocracy was launched by a vocal young group calling themselves the Dalit (downtrodden) Panthers. Like the Naxalites elsewhere in the country, they support the landless labourers, but their principal object is the elimination of caste inequality. Writers and poets within the group focussed attention on the injustices practised for centuries against the Harijans. Theirs is a plea for a transformation in social attitudes commensurate with the legislation that decrees absolute equality.

One of the best known of the Dalit poets is Daya Pawar. In 1982, Bhaskar Chandavarkar who taught music at the Pune Film Institute and composed the music for many of the "new" films, received an NFDC loan to make his own film *Atyachar* (Tyranny). It is based on Daya Pawar's memoirs. The strong content, however, is not supported by an equally strong cinematic treatment. It is nonetheless significant for what it has to say. The poet's experience of the impotence and frustration of being born into a Mahar (an Untouchable) community, finding that education is a double-edged sword cutting him off from both his own people and the upper classes. Called an "educated swine" by the latter, he is trapped in an impossible situation when his own community also rejects him.

Godam (The Warehouse) 1984, another NFDC-financed film, was the first foray into cinema by the writer Dilip Chitre. It is based on a short story by Bhau Padhye, a leading Marathi novelist. Stylistically more innovative than *Atyachar* (both films are in Marathi), it plays on reality and fantasy with three characters isolated from the outside world. A teen-age bride takes refuge in a warehouse after killing her lecherous, perverted father-in-law; a government official in charge of the warehouse is attracted to her but is more concerned about his position; a fatherly peon protects her. The premise has great possibilities but shows the weaknesses inherent in the lack of a technical formation in cinema.

As people from different disciplines found themselves being seduced by the cinema, with opportunities opening up financially, Nachiket and Jayoo Patwardhan, a husband-and-wife team of practising architects in Pune, also applied to the NFDC for a loan. With it, they made *22 June 1897* in 1979. It is the reconstruction (in Marathi) of a violent historical episode, the murder of a British officer by the Chapekar brothers in Pune, their subsequent trial and death sentence. It is a bloody chapter of British repression, intrigue, betrayal and death. Its strong patriotic fervour made a deep impression, but the slow, deliberate style goes ill with a story in which pace and action are called for. More significantly, although it expresses the horror of colonial rule, the message that emerges is one of Hindu revivalism as the antidote to British rule, which gets extended to Christianity itself. This is a graphic instance of the dangers in the lack of a true understanding of cinema, when the intention gets insidiously subverted by the style. All the same, it remains one of the few films that takes recent history as the subject, and for that alone it is important.

It took them several more years to produce their second film *Anant Yatra* (The Return of Godbole) in 1985. In an original script they wrote themselves, this time in Hindi, the Patwardhans take a humourous, witty, perceptive look at the contemporary, affluent urban scene. Through the fantasies and adventures of a Bombay executive suffering from the ill effects of success, they satirize different aspects of modern society. "We feel very strongly that advertising and consumerism are dangerous and creating a society which is imitative of a Western life style," they say. But rather than solemnity they choose comedy in which to cloak their concern. Relationships between wife and husband, children and parents, corruption and the pressures of consumerism all come obliquely into this delightful, wish-fulfilment fairy tale complete with a Mr. Jaduwala (magic-man, wonderfully played by Naseeruddin Shah) who can make dreams come true. Woody Allen and the forties Hollywood classic *The Secret Life of Walter Mitty* plus a Japanese short story about a figure that emerges from a painting, provided the inspiration for a film that is thoroughly Indian in tone and texture. The tone is light, mocking — a far cry from the frequently self-conscious seriousness usually associated with "good" cinema.

Nachiket and Jayoo Patwardhan's ANANT YATRA. 1985

6   EXPLORING SOCIAL CODES

The commercial success of this "middle-of-the road" cinema had started to challenge the sovereignty of the popular cinema. "Serious" directors were using the industry's stars, with Shashi Kapoor leading the way as both producer and actor. In the seventies, he also built the beautiful little Prithvi Theatre, named after his illustrious father Prithviraj Kapoor. A theatre and film actor in the thirties, he was the patriarch of the Kapoor family which has dominated the cinema since the beginning of sound. Shashi Kapoor has acted in films directed by brother Raj, among hundreds of others, and is still a sought-after star. But his major contribution has undoubtedly been as producer of some of the new films, and as the founder, with wife Jennifer Kendal, of the Prithvi Theatre. For the bright young actors it has been a godsend, giving them the possibility of continuing with theatre in the heart of Juhu, where most of the big film studios of Bombay are located, while acting in films. These actors and actresses, many of them trained at the National School of Drama in Delhi or the Pune Film Institute, most of them like Naseeruddin Shah, Om Puri, Shabana Azmi, Smita Patil and Kulbhushan Kharbanda introduced into films by Benegal, move as easily between theatre and film as between the serious and the commercial cinema. Their success in the former opened up opportunities in the latter. This in turn aroused audience interest in the "good" cinema.

In 1979, a year before *Aakrosh*, Vinod Pande made *Ek Baar Phir* (One More Time), with private funding. This first feature film followed many years of making short films and commercials in London. *Ek Baar Phir,* though the style is simple, brought a touch of urban contemporaneity to the content and the character of the woman in the popular film for whom there are no choices and no decisions, and reflected the growth of a new thinking among women themselves. More and more women were working, and their emerging economic independence served to focus attention on their position and the societal attitudes which had for so long dictated it. Vinod Pande's years in the West, and exposure to both this new awareness and the cinema that expressed it, must have influenced the shape of the film he made. In it, a married woman whose tastes, inclinations and values, are the antithesis of her film-star husband's, accompanies him to London where his current film is to be shot. Away from the confines of home and the grip of the family, she has the solitude and the time for introspection as well as for pursuing her own latent interests. She joins art classes, falls in love with a fellow student and actually goes to bed with him. This act, so novel and daring in the Indian cinema, and the turmoil it creates in her are handled with economy and sensitivity. Her feelings are hopelessly divided between her duty as a Hindu wife and her own preferences. The

Shabana Azmi in Vinod Pande's YEH NAZDEEKIYAN. 1983

other man represents not only love but also freedom from a claustrophobic existence. Her final decision to leave the husband is a tribute to the director's courage in breaking the traditional code of screen behaviour in a film that did aim for a large audience. It also proved that the audience had advanced further in its thinking than the filmmakers were aware of. Or that the films of Mrinal Sen, Basu Chatterjee and Shyam Benegal had brought a middle-class audience back into the theatres. To play the role of the young woman, Vinod Pande brought Deepti Naval from New York where she was living. With little experience of acting, she played essentially herself in the film. What it suffered in lack of professional polish in the performances and technique, it made up for in a transparent sincerity and integrity. Pande's next film *Yeh Nazdeekiyan* (Intimacies) was released in the same year, 1983, as Mahesh Bhatt's *Arth* (The Meaning of Life). There are interesting parallels in the two films, indicative of the polarity in the personal and therefore cinematic approach of the two directors. The premise is the same; husband and wife (no children); husband falls in love with another woman met through professional activities (In *Yeh Nazdeekiyan* he is an advertising executive, she is a model; in *Arth* he is a film director, she is an actress) and is propelled by his obsession to leave the wife. In neither case does the relationship prove satisfying. The wife in both films (Shabana Azmi) is very sympathetically drawn in her determination to make something of herself and her life. In neither film does she take easy refuge in another marriage even when it is proposed; the similarity ends. *Yeh Nazdeekiyan* is an open, light, sunny film, a "good" commercial with an upbeat ending. No villains, no vamps. The other woman, played with zest and a hint of sadness, by the lovely star Parveen Babi, is deliriously in love. When she realises that the man she has come to live with is still in love with his wife, she accepts it with regret but no bitterness, recognising that for him it was an infatuation that has ended. She leaves him. Never for one moment is there a sign of the conventional temptress. The husband and wife meet again. They may or may not come together; the question is left open. *Arth,* on the other hand, is full of dark undercurrents. Mahesh Bhatt, its director, had earlier made two out-and-out commercial films. A combination of circumstances, an event in his own life, the altered atmosphere of the film scene and the change in social attitudes took him into a different direction altogether. But in *Arth,* the other woman is played with bitter intensity by Smita Patil, her dress and behaviour evincing the familiar iconography of the vamp. The vague psychological explanations offered ratify the accepted viewpoint. Her hysteria appears to stem from a longing for marriage. Her neurosis prevents her from accepting it because, she says: "If he could leave his wife for me, he can leave me for another woman." The bemused man (Kulbhushan Kharbanda), quite unable to cope with the morbidity, is sent away. He seeks a reconciliation with his wife who, in yet another twist (acclaimed by the women in the audience), asks him a question unthinkable in earlier days— "If I had done what you have, would you take me back?" Too honest to lie, he acknowledges that he would not, and the wife too walks out of his life. The sympathy of the audience is unconsciously directed towards the man, a helpless pawn in a game whose rules are beyond him. The text is full of ambiguities. Initially in a state of shock at finding herself alone, the wife pulls herself together and learns to value her independence. She meets another man who falls deeply in love with her. Although warmed by his caring, she rejects marriage, perhaps fearing a repetition of the earlier painful experience. But she takes on full responsibility for her maid-servant's little daughter. She adopts the child when its mother is taken away to prison after having killed her husband. The implication is clear; fulfilment for a woman lies in being either a wife or, better still, a mother. Although, or perhaps because, the sub-text is conservative, the audience, particularly the women, ensured the success of the film by identifying with the wife. The deep-rooted belief that motherhood is the culmination of woman's achievement is echoed in the film. Seen in this light, the radicalism in the rejection of a husband is tempered in a most satisfying manner.

Mahesh Bhatt's next film *Saaransh* (The Essence), 1984, is set against a background of blatantly unscrupulous and increasingly violence-prone political functioning. But it is so overstated that it is reduced to a caricature. In the foreground is an elderly couple whose only son has been killed in a mugging incident in New York. The mother's overwhelming grief finds strange relief in the conviction that the child their unmarried young woman tenant is expecting, is the son taking birth again. The idea lends itself to a powerful and fascinating exploration of the roots of such beliefs. Satyajit Ray raised superstition to tragic and mythic dimensions in *Devi* (1960). The expressionist style of *Saaransh* has moments of genuine tragedy as the rationalist husband tries to reason with his overwrought wife. The fine performances by Rohini Hattangady (Kasturba in Richard Attenborough's *Gandhi)* and Anupam Kher, both from the National School of Drama, are a glaring contrast to the gimmickry of the rest of the film. The corrupt politician-father appears like the stereotype of the familiar screen villain. He is surrounded by a bunch of goons prepared to terrorize or even kill indiscriminately. The son is as terrified of his father as the spineless doctor, following orders blindly. Violence is in the air, the setting against which individual tragedy tears apart the gentle lives of decent ordinary people. But the film seems to have no real centre. There is little attempt to combine all the different elements and styles into an integrated whole. At best, it is a perfunctory censure of superstition; at worst a playing upon very real fears to manipulate audience susceptibilities, with attacks on corruption and retrograde attitudes towards women thrown in for good measure.

Among a section of newly-arrived filmmakers, the impatience with opposing categories of "art" and "commerce" was being openly articulated. Sai Paranjpye, with a multimedia background in theatre, television, radio and writing, expressed it in no uncertain terms both verbally and in the films she made. "There is an unfortunate distinction in India, between Good cinema and Commercial cinema. We have a strange unwritten code. The artistically-made film should not succeed at the box office, the commercial film must never make sense. The time has come to challenge these norms. I believe in good cinema and I also believe in having an audience for my films. I would never compromise my aesthetic values or commonsense in order to ensure commercial success. But then, I feel that is no longer necessary."* Her first film *Sparsh* (The Touch) was made in 1978, but disagreements with the producer held up distribution until 1984 after two other films by her had been released and enthusiastically received. The script for *Sparsh,* which she wrote herself, was expanded from a television documentary she had made on the Blind School in Delhi. It is a quiet, gentle love story between the blind principal of the school and a beautiful, grieving widow (Shabana Azmi and Naseeruddin Shah). Two people, hurt by life in different ways, eventually overcome pride and pain to come together. In the scenes with the blind children, as mischievous as normal children, with the same laughter and tears, tricks and games, are glimpses of the humour and comedy which came to the fore later in *Chashme Buddoor* (Touch Wood) 1980, and *Katha* (Fable) 1983. Comedy is clearly Paranjpye's forte and she stays within the genre. Light and breezy in *Chashme Buddoor*, where three young men sharing a room fall secretly in love with the same girl, it takes a slightly cynical twist in *Katha,* an allegory on the-hare-and-the-tortoise theme. But in Paranjpye's version, although the slow and steady tortoise (Naseeruddin Shah) wins out against the flashy hare (Farooque Shaikh), it is a doubtful victory. In the world of the *chawl,* the meek do not automatically inherit the earth. Virtue might prevail but only after the non-virtuous have had their fun. Deepti Naval is the object of her shy neighbour's silent love, and his smooth-talking friend's passing

---

* *Indian Cinema,* 1982-83, Directorate of Film Festivals, New Delhi 1983, p. 96.

fancy. Despite Sai Paranjpye's own strong, independent outlook, the viewpoint in her films is still the man's; the woman remains the object acted upon.

Sai Paranjpye's opinion that "popular cinema can also be good cinema" is endorsed by Shekhar Kapur whose *Masoom* (The Innocent One), 1982, once again with Naseeruddin Shah and Shabana Azmi, is a Hindi version of *Man, Woman and Child.* "I never wanted to make art films", Kapur says. "I wanted to do a good film which would also be financially viable. When *Masoom* proved successful, I felt like a free person."* Offers to produce, finance and distribute poured in. The question was what to do next. One thing was certain. It would have to be a film with mass audience appeal, following in the usual success formula. The freedom, therefore, is only within certain parameters. For the directors committed to another kind of cinema, it is far away. The NFDC can provide funds for a first film but if it never gets playing time in theatres for paying audiences, the prestige it might and frequently does acquire, will not necessarily give its maker another chance. That is one reason why some filmmakers have changed direction and objectives mid-stream. Unfortunately, this inhibits both original, innovative talents and audiences from growing.

Pande and Bhatt, Paranjpye and Kapur, had found their own finance for the films they made. But Muzaffar Ali obtained a loan from the NFDC for his first film *Gaman* in 1979. Muzaffar Ali was a painter by choice, an executive with Air India by profession when he too was caught up in the new excitement over the cinema. He wrote, produced, directed and did the art direction himself, taking Smita Patil and Farooque Shaikh as his actors and the great Jaidev from the film industry as his music director. In stark images he paints the life of rural migrants to the city of dreams, Bombay. The heartbreak, the loneliness of those who come away, and of the wives and families left behind, is leavened with humour as a young couple seek private spaces for courtship in the crowded, bustling metropolis. But tragedy is inherent in the situation. The film won him prestige but no real future.

* To the author   Sai Paranjpye's CHASHME BUDDOOR, 1980

Ali belongs to Lucknow, the scion of an aristocratic family, and returned to it for the setting of his next film three years later, *Umrao Jaan.* It is the story of one of the most famous courtesans of the century on whose autobiography the film is based. Exquisite images, each frame a painting, follow each other. The authenticity of the milieu is recreated through superb costumes and jewellery, evocative music (composed this time by Khayyam, another celebrated

Muzzaffar Ali's UMRAO JAAN. 1982

musician from the industry), the palaces of the *nawabs* and the "salons" of the courtesans where poetry and dance, wit and elegance hold men captive. Unfortunately, the loveliness lacks pace and vigour. The result is a series of tableaux from which the characters never really emerge with any sharpness. However, it brought "art" and "commerce" together in the person of the star Rekha, who played the main role. It won her the national best actress award, breaking into the monopoly of the "new cinema's" favourite actors and actresses.

Muzaffar Ali has not found it easy to attract audiences or raise finances for his films. *Gaman* lacked the technical finish of its contemporaries, although it captured a mood and treated an entirely new theme with sensitivity. *Umrao Jaan* found favour with middle-class audiences but not in large enough numbers to tempt private producers looking for big profits. He has just completed a third film *Anjuman* with support from the Uttar Pradesh Government (Lucknow is its capital). But he seems still to be feeling his way in the medium of cinema.

The film-institute graduates with a solid technical background arrive from their training fairly clear about where they want to go. Several of them chose to work in the mainstream soon after graduation. Others are trying to tread a middle path, with finance raised from independent sources. The Institute label has come to stand for technical competence even within the hard-nosed world of commercial cinema. Aruna and Vikas Desai met and married at the film institute, became a sought-after editing team and directed three films together as *Arunavikas,* before deciding to pursue separate directorial careers. The dramatic narrative is their chosen form, so far. *Shaque* (Suspicion), 1979, is a murder mystery. They try and stay within the genre as defined by the Western cinema, but introduce a few elements to make it more palatable to Indian audiences. In the process they, unwittingly, sustain the conventional image of the woman as non-rational, governed primarily by emotion. The husband-wife relationship (Shabana Azmi and the hugely popular star Vinod Khanna) is portrayed at moments with uncommon sensitivity and understanding. *Gehrayee* (The Depths), 1981, carries forward their interest in exploring genres, in this case possession by spirits. An urban, affluent family with warm affectionate relationships between the parents and two teenage children, is shaken to the core when the school-going daughter is suddenly "possessed". Through the film, Aruna and Vikas try to get at the source of the innumerable stories in India of strange, inexplicable happenings which defy scientific explanations and yet cannot be dismissed as mumbo-jumbo. Every incident, the directors say, is based on the actual experiences of people they have met. Aruna has vivid childhood recollections of voodoo-like figures stuck with pins found in the garden of her Bangalore home, of limes suddenly appearing and disappearing as they do in the film. Vikas went to Gangapur where those possessed by spirits go for cures through tantric rituals. The film encourages rational discussion on such occurrences without in any way reinforcing superstitious fears. Their third film *Situm* is in the process of completion.

Blind, superstitious belief as part of an ancient tradition or unscrupulously fostered as a way of keeping the ignorant permanently acquiescent, is a theme being tackled by number of filmmakers. Satyajit Ray led the way, as usual, with *Devi,* Shyam Benegal took it up in *Kondura,* Mahesh Bhatt in *Saaransh.* Arunavikas, Biplab Roy Chowdhury and Amol Palekar are among those that followed.

Biplab Roy Chowdhury had made one film in Bengali, *Barna Bibarna* (Faded Colours) and one in Oriya, *Chilika Teerey* (The Banks of the Chilika) before embarking on *Shodh* (The Search) in Hindi in 1979 and giving Om Puri his first major role. It is an adaption of a story by Sunil Gangopadhyay, author of Satyajit Ray's *Aranyer Din Ratri* and *Pratidwandi.* Starvation subsistence in a village, superstition fed by tales of magic and supernatural happenings, are its setting. Surendra (Om Puri) who had run away from the village, terrified by the powerful landowner, his mother dead, his father murdered by ghosts, so the villagers are led to believe,

Amol Palekar's AKRIET. 1981

returns an angry young man. He is fired by determination to explode the myths of ghosts and magic which are cleverly used to keep the villagers cowed and submissive. Every night he roams the village, offering a reward to anyone who can produce a ghost. The sum grows from one to one hundred rupees. Hunger, beyond the limits of endurance, leads to desperation. An old man eagerly awaits death so his son can claim the reward. When he is shown a girl supposedly possessed by a spirit as proof of the ghost's presence and asked to pay up the money, Surendra treats the girl for hysteria. The myth is exploded. But exploitation and misery continue.

The film hovers uneasily between allegory and simple narrative. Despite its structural weaknesses, it is a film of bitter protest, not a traditional picture of exploitation and misery. Roy Chowdhury's next film *Spandan* (Heartbeat), 1982, has a screenplay by Vijay Tendulkar. In a city, poverty drives a young man to steal cadavers to keep his family alive. Aparna Sen plays Amol Palekar's wife but the film does not rise above commonplace treatment of an intriguing idea.

In 1981, Amol Palekar, introduced into films by Basu Chatterjee in *Rajnigandha* and making a respectable place for himself as an actor in both the new and the commercial cinema, directed his own film in Marathi. He and his wife Chitra, both theatre actors by preference, play the main roles in *Akriet* (Misbegotten). The theme again is superstitious belief carried to the extreme form of human sacrifice of young virgins which, the wife is promised, will achieve her purpose. The subject is powerful, the treatment somewhat obvious and amateurish. In the next film *Ankahee* (The Unspoken) made in 1984 in Hindi, Deepti Naval plays the main role opposite Amol Palekar. It is based on a Marathi play by the poet C.T. Khanolkar. Palekar's handling of cinema shows a marked development since his first film and the voice of the great classical singer Bhimsen Joshi with the music of Jaidev, is beautiful. The theme is still superstition, but in an urban, middle-class milieu. Nandu's father, a middle-class city dweller, is an astrologer. He predicts that Nandu's wife is destined to die in child-birth. Nandu dismisses this prediction as so much mumbo-jumbo but evidence around him eats into his rational outlook. He begins to dread marrying his beloved, Sushma, and connives with his father to marry another girl who is slightly retarded. Sushma deplores the callousness of the plan. Nandu does not consummate the marriage for a long time. However, eventually, he does sleep with his wife who becomes pregnant, and a relationship develops between them. A repentant Nandu unburdens himself to his now cured wife and she, placing her faith in the prediction, grateful for the happiness she has had, prepares to die. In the end, the wife survives the birth of her child while Sushma commits suicide. Palekar questions the blind faith in predictions and subtly criticises the susceptibility that allows fear of the future to invade the joys of the present. What he places under scrutiny is not superstition *per se,* but the fragility of human faith and endurance. Although the sub-stratum of the film could have been made slightly more clear, it is interesting in its questioning of Indian acceptance and fear of, as well as surrender to, the unknown.

In 1984 Vijaya Mehta, a distinguished theatre director and actress (she plays a major role in Nihalani's *Party*), also turned filmmaker, using another incident in history but social, not political. She takes as the subject of *Smriti Chitre* (Memory Episodes), 1983, also in Marathi, the lives of the Reverend Narayan Vaman Tilak and his wife Laxmibai at the turn of the century. Married, according to the prevalent custom, at the age of eleven, Laxmibai educated herself at a comparatively late age, initially pushed into it at her husband's insistence. When he, a Brahmin scholar, converted to Christianity in 1895, she found herself trapped between traditional loyalty to her husband and her own orthodoxy. She continued a Hindu until she had what she calls "a revelation" in her memoirs, which forms the basis of the film. She begins to see that religion and caste are man-made, and turns totally secular in her beliefs. The rough, black-and-white texture of the film, originally made in 16 mm for television, and the rather awkward syntax, detract only marginally from its simple sincerity.

The technical control in many of these films may be uneven, but they show a fertile imagination and a passionate interest in cinema as much as in society. Skills can be acquired through experience if not formal training. In the meantime, the themes and the subjects are taking the contemporary cinema into an expanding area. That is an exciting adventure in itself.

7   **BENGAL'S SECOND BREATH**

The films made in Hindi, not being restricted to a single linguistic zone, have a larger national and frequently urban perspective. Those in the various regional languages are of greater local interest and require a deeper knowledge of cultural and social codes to decipher their meaning fully. Bengal has always been the home of revolutionary fervour and intellectual ferment. In the late sixties, Bengal was riven by political strife. A United-Front government led by the Communist Party (Marxist) but headed by a Gandhian figure (Ajoy Mukherjee) was elected to power in March 1967. By November of the same year discussions within the Front led to desertions. The Party's reluctance to prove its majority and right to rule led to the dismissal of the Assembly and the imposition of President's rule. Prolonged agitation followed. In 1969, the United Front returned to power with a larger majority and in a repetition of the earlier situation, fell under the weight of its contradictions within a year. Another period of confusion ended with the election of a Congress government which ruled from 1972 to 1977, followed once again by the United Front in the '77 elections. Since that time it has succeeded in retaining its majority.

In this political instability the quality of life in Bengal deteriorated steadily. With it came social unrest and increasing politicisation, particularly among the students. In 1967, an armed struggle was launched in Naxalbari in North West Bengal by the Communist Party (Marxist-Leninist (CPM-L) and was subjected to brutal attempts to suppress it by the police. But the struggle only intensified. Unlike the other two parties— the Communist Party of India (CPI) and the Communist Party Marxist (CPM)— the CPM-L rejects parliamentary politics for armed revolution. The Naxalbari uprising has been described as an Indian experiment in Maoism. Since the movement started, those subscribing to this ideology are referred to as Naxalites.

Naxalbari, plus contemporary international events— the Vietnam war, the May 1968 revolution in Paris— had a greater fall-out in Calcutta then elsewhere in the country.

The vitality and resilience of the Calcuttans, however, cannot be stifled. They find ways of coping that show imagination, verve and a sense of humour. A recent happening illustrates their approach to life. The telephone system is the bane of most people's lives all over India, but in Calcutta it has virtually ceased pretending to function. Early in 1985, a funeral ceremony was held for the death of the telephone in front of the building housing the telephone administration. Rites were performed with appropriate solemnity by a genuine *pandit*, and prayers were chanted for the peace of the departed soul, to the vociferous approval of the large congregation.

In the late sixties, Universities became seats more of revolutionary fervour than of learning. Buddhadeb Dasgupta went from University to teach economics in a Calcutta college during eight turbulent years through the sixties and early seventies. He also wrote poetry; three collections of verse were published. But poetry has its limitations when the flame of youth and anger burns brightly, when all around you is despair, destruction and cynicism. Film was the obvious medium that could contain all these and convey them most powerfully to large numbers of people. Dasgupta made three documentaries before his first feature *Dooratwa* (The Distance), 1978. To the human story of Sirshendu Mukhopadhyay he added a socio-political dimension. The distance narrows, grows and narrows again between husband and wife, both fighting their separate battles against exploitation, she as a woman, he as a revolutionary dismayed by the disarray of the radical political movement. Despite the lack of a formal film education, Dasgupta found a quiet style that captured the essence of the characters' inner world where the silences are not only eloquent but also explosive.

In *Neem Annapurna* (Bitter Morsel) 1979, the anger is more bitter. The progressive impoverishment of a family as the father loses his job in a small-town factory in Bengal. The move to Bombay, the dreams that turn sour as poverty catches them by the throat, the hunger that drives husband and wife and the two growing daughters into petty theft and culminates in murder. The wife kills a beggar for his bag of rice. It is a merciless reminder of the dregs of existence which is one of the levels at which India subsists. For many of the new filmmakers, grinding poverty and exploitation are in the foreground of at least one of their films. Perhaps it

Buddhadeb Dasgupta's GRIHA YUDDHA. 1982

is an exorcism of guilt for their own relatively affluent circumstances, perhaps a reaction to the commercial cinema's opulence and false sentimentalising of poverty as something noble and pure. Here is the grimness of real poverty, they seem to be saying. It is bleak, it is utterly dehumanising. Their films refuse to absolve the audience from a share in the collective guilt for such a situation.

With *Grihajuddha* (The Crossroad) 1982, Buddhadeb Dasgupta returns to the middle-class moral and political crisis, a background and condition he knows best. It is an extension of his earlier concern in *Dooratwa*. Calcutta is the setting, its theme the erosion of idealism and faith in revolutionary politics, growing violence, and the courage of the young woman who struggled and waited and then rejected the man she loved because her convictions withstood the trials while he gave up. No overt anger but impressive inner strength. Memorable moments as when the camera follows Anjan Dutt, the renegade revolutionary, through the rooms of the new apartment he has taken where he waits for Mamata Shanker whom he expects to marry. The emptiness of the rooms reflects the emptiness within him. As he walks aimlessly, restlessly, the camera follows him, probing, thrusting, forcing him to look within himself, refusing to allow him to escape from his sense of guilt and failure, and to run away from himself as he ran away from commitment. Mamata Shanker played the main role in *Dooratwa* as well and, thematically, *Grihajuddha* is the second in what was to become a trilogy. The investigative reporter whose deepening involvement with the story he uncovers and for which he is killed, is played by Goutam Ghose. He brings his own vibrant intensity and attractive presence to a role in which he plays essentially himself. In the same year Dasgupta made *Sheet Grishmer Smriti* (Season's Memoirs) where a play, sponsored by a business house, exposes the very activities of which the company itself is perennially guilty. The sponsors storm out of the theatre leaving the director of the play alone with his dreams.

All of Dasgupta's films have as their central character the solitary individual whose visions are of heroic action but, faced with reality, he falters, and falls. In *Andhi Gali* (Blind Alley), 1984, in Hindi, Dasgupta follows the protagonist of *Grihajuddha* to a life of materialism and exploitation in Bombay; he represents the manner in which the middle class turns its back on the violent reality around, how it flees the main arena of political happenings. It is a reflection of the protagonist himself, as in the earlier films, sickened by his timidity and vacillation when it comes to living up to his convictions. *Andhi Gali,* however, falls into its own trap. Private funding, commercial considerations. Perhaps in treating the decay of idealism and the exploitative nature of middle-class morality, it becomes exploitative itself. The eloquent silences and sensitivity have disappeared along the way. Temporarily, one hopes.

Six years younger than Buddhadeb Dasgupta, Goutam Ghose went through a phase of leftist politics in his student days. Travelling through India for his documentaries and as a photo-journalist gave him direct contact with the reality which lay behind the idealism of student politics. In 1980, the year following Dasgupta's *Neem Annapurna,* Ghose was asked to make a film in Telugu in Andhra Pradesh. Ghose had already made two documentaries, the second of which *Hungry Autumn* in 1976, had won critical acclaim and several awards. Andhra Pradesh was the state where the Telengana movement had been born, and Ghose found a story of the Hindi novelist Krishna Chander on the Telengana revolt of 1948. He wanted to make the film in Hindi but the producers—one of them was B. Narsing Rao—were keen on Telugu, as they felt the subject was of immediate interest to the people who were directly concerned with it. Three months of research in Hyderabad, capital of Andhra Pradesh, and Goutam Ghose produced a scenario he felt was "too sophisticated for its purpose." He re-wrote it to make it into a straight narrative two-and-a-half hours long. It explained "the background, the failure of the movement, what happened to the Communist Party and so on."* *Ma Bhoomi* (Mother Earth) ran continuously for one year in Andhra Pradesh.

The youngest of the contemporary trinity of Bengali filmmakers, united by a similar background and commitment, Ghose has been steadily refining his perceptions and his work. *Dakhal* (The Occupation) 1981, is his second film and the only one, so far, in Bengali. Its tight, compact structure and strong characterisations, are a major development since *Ma Bhoomi*. *Paar* (The Crossing) 1984, is that much further ahead again. *Dakhal* is rural India, nomadic tribes, caste differences, the powerful zamindar (landowner) seeking an alliance with the contemporary representative of power, the law courts, to legitimise his sharp practices. Opposing him this time is a woman (Mamata Shanker). Young, widowed, she takes on the combined strength of the law, traditional vested interests, male power and, fighting for her right to retain her dead husband's land, subdues it. She is no crusader: just an ordinary woman, alone, defenceless, who rejects the submissive role society would thrust upon her. The need to protect her two small children sustains her determination. The men appear as vacillating, weak, gullible, easily bought over, taking recourse to physical violence (setting her miserable hut on fire) to bring her, in vain, to her knees. When the repentant leader of the tribe she had left to elope with Joga, a peasant from another caste, offers to take her back with them, she chooses to stay and continue her battle. The story is filmed evocatively in black and white by Ghose

Goutam Ghose's DAKHAL, 1981

* The Telengana movement 1944-51, was the first widespread, sustained armed struggle of peasants in recent times against feudal oppression. During the movement, led by the Communist Party of India, a large area was administered by the peasants' representatives. Telengana was originally a part of Hyderabad State ruled by the Nizam. The princely state was merged with the rest of India after Independence in 1947, following police action by the Central Government. The liquidation of the Movement followed. The city of Hyderabad is now the capital of the State of Andhra Pradesh.

himself, with no concessions to relieve the starkness of the age-old tale of the exploitation of the weak, or the harshness of the environment in which it is practised.

Paar (in Hindi) moves from the village to the city. It is less organically structured than *Dakhal.* There is only a very tenuous link between its two halves as we move with the protagonists (Shabana Azmi and Naseeruddin Shah- who else!) from the misery of a known habitat (the village) into the misery of the unknown big city (Calcutta). But the latter half transcends the documentary realism of the beginning to become a metaphor for the nobility of the human spirit. It has refreshing moments of humour which vary the pitch, giving it richness and suppleness; Goutam Ghose's control is growing. In pouring rain the couple sleep on the city's pavements in the semi-shelter of doorways, along with a friend they have acquired in their flight from persecution in the village. A drunken passerby shakes the wife awake and makes lewd advances. Those who sleep on the street must expect to be picked up, is the cynically implied comment. The friend awakes and chases the man in fury. A car careens to a stop. Out roll a bunch of affluent young men, equally inebriated. Dancing wildly in the rain, they try to draw the bewildered villager into their circle to celebrate India's victory in the World Cup (India had just won the World Cup at the cricket championship in London and the entire country was jubilant). The solemnity and earnestness of most filmmakers of the realist school is rarely relieved by such flashes of humour or comment that lie outside the immediate diegesis of the film.

For Utpalendu Chakraborty life is real, life is earnest, so is anger. His films come closest to the concept of the Third Cinema as "that cinema of the Third World which stands opposed to imperialism and class oppression in all their ramifications and manifestations."* Also in 1980, he made his short film *Mukti Chai* (We Want Liberation). Initially wanting to study art, he was obliged by parental pressure into working instead for a degree in modern history at the university. From art to politics. Participating in the Calcutta food riots in 1966 when he was just eighteen, he was arrested in a demonstration against Robert McNamara, then President of the World Bank. After being released from jail he became an active member of the Communist Party of India (Marxist-Leninist) and under a party directive moved among the tribals of Bengal-Bihar-Orissa (three contiguous States) as a non-formal teacher. Faced with the reality of absolute deprivation and unending exploitation, he returned to the city determined to make others confront the truth and the terror. Short stories proved unsatisfying, almost as limited in their reach and impact as poetry. He borrowed a movie camera and the result was *Mukti Chai,* a 50-minute documentary on the mass movement for the release of political prisoners. More a tract than a film it nevertheless crystallised his ideas on the role and function of cinema. *Moyna Tadanta* (Post Mortem) was made the following year, based on his own short story about a poor young tribal man thought to have committed suicide. The post mortem reveals the actual cause of death to have been starvation. According to Utpalendu, Mrinal Sen had planned to make this film, and when he abandoned the idea, Chakraborty did it himself, half the total budget given to him as a grant by the West Bengal government.

Chokh (The Eye) in 1982 showed that Chakraborty was learning to handle the cinema with growing dexterity. But the substance still takes precedence over the style. Jadunath, the leader of the workers in a Calcutta factory, framed for a murder he did not commit, is condemned to death. He wills his eyes to a blind colleague but the business magnate who, it turns out, had been responsible for the events that led to the labour leader's conviction, wants the Eye Bank to give them to him for his son. Discovering later that they have been donated by Jadunath, he tries

---

* Teshome H. Gabriel, op cit p. 2

Utpalendu Chakraborty's CHOKH. 1982

various tactics to have them destroyed; they have become symbolic of the workers' fighting spirit. The film ends with a demonstration by the workers demanding the eyes for their colleague, as Jadunath is driven to his appointment with the hangman. *Chokh* has some embarrassingly obvious moments which arise principally out of its shooting style. At the same time it has moments of extraordinary intensity as when Om Puri (as Jadunath), faces death with agonising fear, alone in his prison cell the night before he must hang. Or at the end when his wife (Srila Mazumdar) takes the hand of the blind worker for whom her husband has willed his eyes, to lead the demonstration against the management. *Chokh* was entirely financed and produced by the West Bengal government, as were *Dakhal* and *Grihajuddha*. Such support undoubtedly made it easier for all three directors to make their kind of films without considerations of commercial viability. The sole inhibiting factor is language. Goutam Ghose made *Paar* in Hindi with private financing. Despite the many awards and publicity the film has had, distribution is not easy. *Grihajuddha* and *Chokh* were in Bengali, and the West Bengal Government itself distributed them. Utpalendu Chakraborty, however, is outspoken in his views — "I am committed to the struggle of the working class which has been frequently bluffed and betrayed by the so-called leaders of Communist or Marxist parties... I have no respect for the leadership but I have an immense amount of respect for the class of people these leaders claim to represent." This in spite of the help he has received from the Left Front Government of his State. His response is — "Simply by providing finances they cannot convince me into propagating their ideology. I can take their money and make a film which is highly critical of them. I am not a purchaseable commodity. It is true I received money from the Left Front Government but it is not my intention to toe their line."[*] In terms of content, in their desire to come to grips with social and political realities these films have strong links with Mrinal Sen and Ritwik Ghatak. With a common background and a shared initial premise, they show marked differences. For Utpalendu, film becomes a weapon to be used for denouncing what is wrong. For Buddhadeb, it is a way "to point a finger at the erratic past and wake our people to the dangerous role of the so-called intellectual middle-classes."[*] Goutam Ghose is less directly interested in using cinema as a message carrier, more concerned about people, more of an optimist. "I believe in social change, I believe in history, in a scientific view of history. It will change, it is changing. I feel it is very important to communicate hope."

Satyajit Ray, Mrinal Sen and Ritwik Ghatak have been seminal influences on Bengal's second wave, particularly Ray "for the musical structure of his films." But for Goutam Ghose the major influence has been Orson Welles, despite his large exposure to European cinema and European literature through his professor-father. Ray is like a father figure. "He watches our films very carefully, offers many very good suggestions, sometimes analysing them shot by shot," Utpalendu Chakraborty said, and dedicated *Chokh* to Ray. In 1984 he went on to make a half-hour documentary on "The Music of Satyajit Ray". But the influence of Ray is seen most clearly in the work of Aparna Sen. Daughter of Chidananda Das Gupta, she was thirteen when she acted (as Mrinmoyee) in Ray's *Teen Kanya*. It was a brief interruption of her studies, and she went on to finish University before taking seriously to acting with distinction in the Bengali cinema — including other Ray and Mrinal Sen films. Literature, as with many Bengalis, was a continuing interest, and impeccable taste "made of a thousand distastes". It was in memory of her Shakespeare teacher at school that she started writing a short story. It developed into the screenplay of her *36 Chowringhee Lane* which she made in English in 1981. The relationship of an ageing, lonely, proud, Anglo-Indian school-teacher with a former student and her boy-friend, is portrayed with compassion and touches of humour. Life is hard, but there are

---

[*] Utpalendu Chakraborty in an interview with S.N.M. Abdi & Harsha Dave, the Sunday Observer, Bombay, May 15-21, 1983.

moments of joy and laughter and companionship that make it well worthwhile. There are delicious scenes in this film as when the young couple embrace in the taxi and the girl pulls away with an indignant gesture at the cab driver enjoying the — for India — unusual spectacle in the driving mirror. Kissing, taboo in the popular cinema until very recently, is something from which the new filmmakers also shy away. But *Chowringhee Lane* has a single, very delicately handled, kissing scene. Another time the couple finally find themselves alone in the flat the school teacher lends them (ostensibly so the man can have a quiet, private place to write). After the frustrations of furtive embraces, they have a bedroom to themselves. Lying in bed, the girl suddenly sits up saying— "No. *He* is watching". It is the cat, curious about the unfamiliar activity on its mistress' usually chaste bed! There is the last, poignant scene as the teacher walks away from the Christmas party the now-married couple are hosting. She has not been invited and sees it by chance. It is a moment of terrible hurt and rejection for her. But she straightens her back, pats a stray dog that adopts her, and walks away with it into the night, back to her empty flat. On the sound track is her voice reciting the lines from King Lear:

> Come let's away to prison,
> We two alone will sing like birds i' th' cage...

It could have been embarrassingly sentimental. It is deeply moving, drawing into it the reverberations and the hurt of old age, loneliness, pride, the passing of an era, the fading away of a community that had outlived its history.

Aparna Sen's 36 CHOWRINGHEE LANE. 1981

Aparna Sen, like Satyajit Ray, has been criticised for not making a film about "social problems", for not dealing, in this instance, with the question of Anglo-Indians generally. Her answer is: "The sense of guilt (about social privilege & deprivation) is absolutely justified. I have a sense of guilt, everybody does. But people tend to sublimate it by making a film and thinking that will take care of the problem. It doesn't. Writing about it, talking about it, discussing it, making a film about it, is not going to solve anything. I think I have reflected social conditions in the film and I have tried to do it through one individual instead of being strident. If you want to touch a chord somewhere in people then sloganeering or shaking your fist won't do it."*

Aparna Sen's own acting experience has been a major asset in her style of direction— 36 Chowringhee Lane has a wonderful performance by Jennifer Kendal, the English actress whose husband Shashi Kapoor, produced the film. Aparna Sen says that as the story she wrote started shaping into a film script, it was Jennifer Kendal and no one else she visualised in that role.

After Chowringhee Lane Aparna Sen went back to acting, taking her time to write a script for the second film Paroma which she made in two versions— Bengali and Hindi— in 1985. It became an instant and controversial issue for, this time, she took as its focus the arousal of dormant individuality in a middle-aged, traditional Bengali housewife. Mores were changing rapidly in India; pre- and extra-marital affairs, divorce, even proudly unwed mothers, a part of the urban scene. But few films had dared explore such areas. In Anant Yatra the husband's affair with a young woman even in his fantasy life was considered shocking enough with the Patwardhans' being accused of advocating adultery! In Paroma, a middle-aged mother actually falling in love and going to bed with another man, was something normal audiences found hard to stomach. It strikes at the very heart of familial and social organisation in which the mother-figure occupies an archetypal position that is eternal and unchanging.

The early premise of the film is bold and challenging but is not sustained. Self-realization for the woman comes through the man, through gratification from becoming an object of desire, from breaking out of the anonymous Wife/Mother role. The bewilderment of the extended family when they discover her "duplicity", her reaction to the stress, have not been fully or clearly worked out. Aparna Sen seems more at ease when handling the growth and culmination of the relations between the woman and her young lover. The latter half which concerns the relationships within the family is less assured.

As different from his politically engaged contemporaries as Aparna Sen, is Sandeep Ray. His Phatikchand is another first film in (father) Satyajit's footsteps, but in the childrens' fantasy ones rather than those of the "human document" style.

With story, script and music by Satyajit Ray, it is no wonder that it is cast in the image of his own Felunath spirit. A young boy is kidnapped for ransom. His bumbling kidnappers wreck the get-away car. Two of them are killed, the other two run away, and the boy wakes up with amnesia. His subsequent adventures in the city with the juggler who befriends him, has all the makings of a delightful childrens' fairy tale. But the pace tends to drag, the situations are too long drawn-out to engross you to the expected degree. The signs of talent are apparent, waiting in the wings for a second effort. Sandeep Ray has a sound technical knowledge, and in this first film is far ahead of most other new entrants in the field. For the moment, however, he too has succumbed to the lure of television.

Other filmmakers in Bengal have been treading a middle path for years. Tarun Mazumdar, Hari Dasgupta, Tapan Sinha, Utpal Dutt, Purnendu Pattrea, all belong to an older generation that kept alive the cause of good cinema in a vein that middle-class audiences responded to. Tarun Mazumdar and Utpal Dutt are among those who have profited from the West Bengal government's financing scheme.

* To the author

The first State Government to have financially assisted a film director, the West Bengal government's Department of Information and Cultural Affairs has once again shown what enlightened policy can achieve. In September 1985, it opened the Calcutta Film Centre. The only complex of its kind (the Kerala State Film Development Corporation has a more modest complex in Trivandrum), it has three auditoria, a film library and book-shop, an Archive with viewing rooms for film and video, and a film museum. A colour laboratory with editing rooms is coming up separately. All these years, the best laboratories and studios were in Bombay and Madras. The opening of the Film Centre underlines the importance the West Bengal government accords to the cinema, and signals its intention of restoring to Calcutta its pre-eminence as the country's cultural and film centre.

8

SOUTHERN ARRIVAL

"I would rather be an immortal in theatre than a celebrity in film," Girish Karnad said, twelve years after he entered Indian film history with *Samskara*. He did not make that film but he collaborated on the script, played the main role, and was responsible for getting Pattabhi Rama Reddy interested in producing and directing it. Karnad was then working for the Oxford University Press in Madras; the manuscript he read of the novel *Samskara* was in Kannada, which is the language of the region Karnataka where he comes from; Snehalata Reddy was a member of an amateur theatre group, Madras Players, with which Girish was involved; and Pattabhi Rama Reddy, her husband, was a producer of Telugu films. The wife of the painter S.G. Vasudev who became the art director for *Samskara*, was also a member of Madras Players. At that time, in 1969, there was no "new" movement in film-making in the South, and no Kannada film industry as such at all. A few films were made in Kannada in the studios and laboratories of Madras. *Samskara*, ironically, launched both the New Wave and provided the impetus for the birth of an industry. The novel by U.R. Ananthamurthy was part of a new literary movement in Karnataka. In the fifties and sixties there was both an awakening social consciousness and a cultural renaissance in Karnataka, in which the ideas of the socialist leader Ram Manohar Lohia played a significant part. Pattabhi Rama Reddy and K.S. Karanth participated in the movement. U.R. Ananthamurthy was to write after Lohia's death: "Writing, as I did, under the cultural imperialism of European-born ideas, like many other Indian writers, I was fortunate to have read Lohia for he rooted me in the Indian soil. Those were the days when for the Indian intellectual the unorthodox behaviour of a Ginsberg was revolutionary, whereas Lohia's actions seemed quixotic..... His main importance for literary people consists in his vital criticism of culture in which he neither denounces the past nor extols it, but with great flexibility of mind discriminates between its current alive and sterile expressions...Lohia's caste analysis had helped me to see how the caste system can trap you and thus limit your awareness of life."[*]

Girish Karnad, with his first play *Yayati* (1961) was instrumental in reviving a languishing contemporary Indian theatre. With his second play *Tughlak* (all his plays are in Kannada), in 1964, he achieved national prominence. The cinema that developed in Karnataka, grew out of a fusion of the rebirth of a literary and a theatre movement. *Samskara* (Funeral Rites) was completed in 1970. A strongly anti-caste, anti-Brahmin film, it was at first banned by the

[*] U.R. Ananthamurthy "Contemporary Relevance of Lohia" in *Lohia: Many Faceted Personality*. Lohia|Smarak Samiti. Lucknow, 1984, pp 123-24

Censor Board and, in a not unusual occurrence, went on to win the national award for the best film of the year. In a firmly orthodox, Brahmin-dominated society, the film appeared an almost subversive act. It was, in fact, the start of a series of films across the country which attacked the continuing feudal pattern of rural life, and the passive acceptance of it by a people numbed into silence and apathy. Structurally, as narrative, 't holds together effectively. The lighting, camera angles, particularly in the close-ups of the faces and the way they are grouped together, were remarkable. Shot by an Australian cameraman Tom Cowan who happened to be in India, it has a visual power which only Satyajit Ray and Ritwik Ghatak — less well known at the time — had displayed. The somewhat stilted manner and weak inner rhythm are forgotten in the face of its compelling under-current of intensity. Its lack of professional polish and its technical inadequacies are relatively unimportant considering its mode of production and what it did for the future of cinema in Karnataka. A group of amateurs dedicated to the idea of a film without compromises, its extremely low budget, the shooting on actual location in a village, the immediate recognition it won, make it an important landmark. For Karnad, however, it did not immediately signify the beginning of a new career in cinema. He resigned from Oxford University Press to go and live in a village, study India and write about it. It was the way many young urbanised Indians were beginning to react. Cut off from the "real" India by their Western education, they were becoming aware of a need to rediscover their own tradition and through it, their identity. But it was quickly apparent that *Samskara* had stirred up more than any of those involved with it had realised. The theatre director B.V. Karanth was asked to direct a film based on a very successful Kannada novel by S.L. Byrappa. Knowing little about cinema but attracted by the idea, he proposed to Karnad, a very good friend, that they do it together. So Karnad did not retreat to a village. Instead, he co-directed *Vamsa Vriksha* (The Family Tree) 1971 with Karanth. It was produced by G.V. Iyer who played a role in it, and then went on to direct a number of popular films, before making the controversial, visually stunning *Adi Sankaracharya* in Sanskrit in 1983. *Vamsa Vriksha* places the tyranny of Brahminism and the personal tragedies that result from it, into a more contemporary milieu. With another success on their hands, Karnad and Karanth both found themselves being drawn deeper into films, and Karnataka replaced Bengal as the centre of serious cinema. It was a heady period. Karnad was offered another manuscript, *Kaadu* (The Forest) to film. The first, autobiographical novel of 25-year old, Krishna Anahalli, it was set in a village around 1946-47. And Karanth went on to make his own first — and so far only — independent film, *Chomanadudi* (Chomana's Drum) in 1975. They were to come together one more time in 1977 to co-direct *Godhuli/Tabbaliyu Neenade Magane* (The Hour of the Gods) in two versions, Hindi and Kannada. Brahmin orthodoxy was the target in this as in *Samskara*, Naseeruddin Shah the passionate priest confessing at the end that in his pre-occupation with formal Brahminism he had lost sight of humanity. The confrontation between East and West, modernity and tradition, is embodied by the mute mother and the son who returns home with an American wife; and also by the orthodox young Brahmin priest struggling with his conscience, trying to explain India to the modern young American woman, herself struggling to understand an alien culture. There is no satisfying conclusion, no synthesis achieved, but the first step towards it has been taken. The film is more interesting for what it attempts than for what it actually succeeds in doing.

Kaadu, 1973, with Karanth to do the music and art direction, Govind Nihalani at the camera, shows clearer signs of what Karnad was doing so successfully in his plays. Bothered by his cosmopolitan upbringing, out of touch with a contemporary, authentic Kannada context, all his plays are concerned with myth and history. "The past," he says, "gives you the ability to control what you want to say. A contemporary subject has too many demands." *Kaadu* draws away from the present into the recent past, from Brahminism and the modernity/tradition conflict into the violence of a feudalistic society. Karnad shuns the documentary realism which

Girish Karnad's ONDANONDU KALADILLI. 1978

B.V. Karanth's CHOMANADUDI, 1975

has become the choice of so many "committed" new film makers. The child's world, full of fantasy and fear, and the atmosphere of the forest which separates the two villages are powerfully evoked. Otherwise, technically, the film belongs to a more simplistic era of film-making.

Karnad was, however, working towards something quite different, as his next two films showed. There was a five-year gap between *Kaadu* and *Ondanondu Kaladilli* (Once upon a Time) made in 1978, the year after *Godhuli. Ondanondu Kaladilli,* the only one of his films for which he wrote the script himself, is a martial-arts film set in the thirteenth century in Karnataka, and is a frankly acknowledged homage to Kurosawa. To it, Karnad brings all his zest and enjoyment of cinema as action and colour and movement. His technical mastery had grown considerably in the intervening years. He had moved out of Karnataka to become Director of the Film Institute in 1974-75. In 1976, he acted in Shyam Benegal's *Manthan,* Basu Chatterjee's *Swami* and Sridhar Kshirsagar's *Kanakambara,* and then continued with film making. The year at the Film Institute where, as he says, he was more a student than the Director, gave him the kind of intense, sustained exposure to films that would otherwise have been difficult to come by. It also gave him the opportunity to study film-making systematically. He left because he started "enjoying the job too much", and felt that he would "never be able to write or make another film because the Institute was all-engrossing."* That the experience was fully absorbed is evident in *Ondanondu...* which is a finely-crafted film that brings in all the elements closest to him.

Another six years elapsed before Karnad's next and latest film *Utsav* (Festival) 1984. Six years of acting in Bombay in the heart of the commercial film world; he wrote or collaborated on scripts for Shyam Benegal, *(Bhumika, Kondura, Kalyug),* wrote another play, and continued to act in the most extraordinary variety of films. At the back of his mind was a film he had long wanted to do, based on the 4th century classical Sanskrit play *Mrichchakatika* (The Little Clay Cart). An expensive film to make, *Utsav* was ultimately realised when Shashi Kapoor decided to produce it, playing the main role himself opposite Rekha. Sumptuously mounted, with some genuinely funny moments and Shashi Kapoor in perhaps the best role of his career, it remains a gorgeous set-piece. Rekha has never looked so beautiful, but the authenticity of costumes and setting, the sensuous lighting and camerawork do not succeed in lifting it to a high artistic level. It seems weighed down by its own riches, by the grandeur of its scale. The care lavished on outer reality and to compositions within the frame, overwhelms the characters and relationships. There is no strong inner core to the film, just sheer aesthetic pleasure. The means of production? Perhaps. A larger audience in view? Undoubtedly, given Shashi Kapoor's proclaimed ambition to make "good" films that would be commercially viable. But commercial viability is related, in India at least, to language and budget. *Kaadu* was in black and white, *Ondanondu Kaladilli* in colour, but both were in Kannada, and Karnad knew their audience would be restricted to their language region. The budget had to be kept within reasonable bounds. *Utsav* was in two versions, Hindi and English. It sent the production budget soaring while aiming for both an all-India and an international audience. Karnad had moved far away from his initial point of departure.

Karanth in the meantime, made *Chomanadudi* (Chomana's Drum) in 1975, on a story and screenplay by Dr. K.S. Karanth. Set in the 1930s, it has as its protagonist Chomana, a crusty old man, frustrated by the grinding poverty to which there is no end, filled with rage at the injustice all around him. The only outlet he has is his drum through which he gives vent to his feelings. A priest attempts to convert him to Christianity with the promise of two acres of land. His daughter sleeps with the British overseer of the plantation, and redeems the loan of twenty

* Interview with Girish Karnad in *Indian Cinema Superbazaar,* p. 220.

Girish Kasaravalli's GHATASHRADDHA, 1977

rupees taken years earlier. The payment of the interest alone had kept the entire family toiling for a miserable pittance. Two of Chomana's sons die, one drowns when no one helps him because he is a *harijan*, the other succumbs to cholera. The third son becomes a Christian. When Chomana learns what price his daughter has paid to wipe out the twenty-rupee debt, his disillusionment is complete. He dies. But the sound of his drum lives on, a reminder and a spur to others.

The role of Chomana is brilliantly played by Vasudev Rao, whom Mrinal Sen took later for his Telugu film *Oka Oorie Katha*. The rather simple, static visual style of the film — "I feel it is very important to awaken social consciousness," Karanth says — is compensated by the complex, evocative music he composed for it.

Karanth's training was in both theatre and music. He started out at the age of twelve, playing bit roles in Karnataka's famous Gubbi Theatrical Company which included such future luminaries as G.V. Iyer and Vasudev Rao. When the company closed, moral encouragement and a regular stipend from its owner helped Karanth to complete his studies and leave for Varanasi to work for a Ph.D. on the Indian Stage and Hindi Drama. It was there that he studied North Indian classical music under the great Pandit Onkar Nath Thakur. He joined the National School of Drama in Delhi in 1960 as part of the research for his doctorate. Delhi became his base, and he created the Dishantar group to do plays at a time when interest in modern theatre was at a very early stage. *Vamsa Vriksha* came out of the blue and took him back to Bangalore after a long absence. G.V. Iyer, its producer, ran temporarily short of funds to complete it. Karanth and Karnad found themselves at a loose end, which Karanth put to good use by producing twelve plays in eight months.

At Bangalore University, a Drama and Literature seminar at this time brought together a variety of people. Lankesh and Chandrasekhar Kambhar were both teaching at the university, Karnad and Karanth were waiting to edit *Vamsa Vriksha*, S.G. Vasudev, the painter, arrived from Cholamandal, the Artists Village near Madras. Y.N. Krishnamurthi, editor of *Prajavani*, was a key figure around whom they all gathered. Karanth directed three plays for the seminar: *Oedipus* in which Karnad acted, had been translated into Kannada by Lankesh; *Jo Kumaraswamy* by Kambhar, and *Sankranthi* by Lankesh. It was a turning point in the theatre in Karnataka with spoken Kannada being used for the first time on the stage. In all this turbulence, *Vamsa Vriksha* was completed, and Karanth went on to Bhopal, there to organise the first major theatre workshop. K.S. Karanth agreed to allow *Chomanadudi* to be filmed provided it was directed by B.V. Karanth. With Girish Kasaravalli as his assistant, Karanth made *Chomanadudi* independently. He stayed on in Bangalore, composing music for several films, including Kasaravalli's *Ghatashradha* (The Ritual) as he had done earlier for *Samskara* and *Kaadu*. But *Chomanadudi* was his only independently directed film. He was for a year, Principal of the Adarsh Film Institute (founded in Bangalore in 1973), then moved back to Delhi, this time as Director of the National School of Drama where he stayed for four years. Constitutionally incapable, it seems, of staying too long in one place, he left Delhi for Bhopal to head the Rangmandal Theatre Group, part of the prestigious Bharat Bhavan, the cultural centre set up by the State Government of Madhya Pradesh in its capital city. And there, for the moment, he remains. Film direction, he says, was an accident he would gladly repeat if the opportunity presented itself. But theatre is in his blood.

Karnad and Karanth, with their varied grounding in theatre, literature and music, launched the new cinema in Karnataka. The training at the Film Institute in Pune and the desire to search for the roots of their own traditions and cultures — now seen as a false "regionalism" — sent the graduates back home rather than seek employment in established centres of film. Girish Kasaravalli returned from Pune in 1976 to Bangalore when the interest in serious cinema was at its height. He made *Ghatashradha* in 1977 when he was 26 years old. Written also by U.R.

Prema Karanth's PHANIYAMMA, 1982

Ananthamurthy, *Ghatashraddha* continues the attack on Brahmin orthodoxy. The title signifies the excommunication of "immoral" Brahmin widows by the breaking of an earthen pot symbolising the womb, and Kasaravalli treats it in a ritualistic manner. What could be an emotional story becomes a ritual itself, observed from a distance, simultaneously detached and filled with anger.

The image of women, suppressed and humiliated in society, exploited and humiliated in the popular cinema, was beginning to change in the new cinema. Those who were concerned with social issues were exercised over the treatment meted out to women as to all oppressed groups and communities. Kasaravalli's next film *Akramana* (The Conquest) in 1979 is, however, far removed from the Brahminical tyranny of the past in *Ghatashraddha*. It is a psychological probing into the fears, conflicts and motivations of three young people living in contemporary urban surroundings, but incapable of freeing themselves from heavy, traditional conditions. In 1981 he made *Mooru Darigalu* (Three Paths) where he returns to the continuing victimisation of women, in this case slander, wicked and baseless, which drives the young woman in it to suicide. It is her only means of protest. Neither of these two films, although extremely well shot by another young Institute graduate Shripati R. Bhatt, measure up to *Ghatashraddha* in the dramatic poetry of its images or the economy and fluency of its style. From 1978 to 1985 Kasaravalli was head of the Adarsh Film Institute, a position he took over from Karanth.

Emboldened by the response to the three K's — Karnad, Karanth and Kasaravalli — others also tried their hand at a similar kind of film-making. Sridhar Kshirsagar with a background in advertising films made *Kanakambara* with Girish Karnad playing the main role.

Meanwhile, the State Government of Karnataka had been fired by enthusiasm with the publicity and prestige these films brought to Karnataka. It set up a State Film Development Corporation and started to offer grants and subsidies for films shot either in Kannada or simply within the State itself. It has a fully equipped studio, and editing rooms. It led to a spurt in film-making in general: studios and laboratories came up. From 25 films a year, Kannada cinema jumped to 60 a year. Budgets became bigger, colour the norm. Big budget commercial films began to corner the market. With no increase in the number of theatres, the smaller films stood no chance. Around 1980, the entertainment tax on all films classified "Adult" was doubled. The last blow was the reduction in the subsidy. It spelt death to the low-budget, serious film.

There were other causes also for the sudden decline of the Kannada New Wave. According to Girish Karnad, technical incompetence was a major reason. Everyone thought that to go to a village and make a film was the thing. All the films started looking alike. Problems in a village being basically very limited, they kept repeating themselves — "the whole movement just got bogged down in repetition."

Prema Karanth's lovely *Phaniyamma*, 1982, was perhaps the swan song of the first Kannada New Wave. Married to B.V. Karanth, herself a distinguished theatre director (she spent 3 years as a student at the National School of Drama, two years as a member of the Repertory Company), her interest in films was nurtured through acting, designing costumes and then art direction. She was art director for *Hamsa Geethe* and *Kudure Motte* (in which she and Karanth acted), both made by G.V. Iyer. She also played a lead role in V. Jagannath's *Kadige Hodovaru*. *Phaniyamma* again, has a rural setting, but Prema Karanth in no way reflects the preoccupations of her male contemporaries. It comes closest to *Ghatashraddha* in that it shows the absolute oppression of widows in orthodox Brahminism, but the two approaches are entirely different. *Ghatashraddha* is more formal, purer in style, and through an incident in the life of one woman, makes a larger statement about the plight of all women. At the end, pushed out of her village by an unrelenting, inhuman, male-dominated community, she is left alone, ing near a tree in a wide, hostile space. As the camera pulls back, she merges into the darkness, becoming one with nature, with the tree. *Phaniyamma* is in the humanist tradition. It is a straightforward story that spans the life of one woman from childhood to death and, through her, shows the evolution of society in seventy years. A bright, laughing girl, she is married off as a child to a little boy hardly older than herself. The joyous atmosphere at the doll-like wedding turns quickly into tragedy as the boy-husband dies of snake-bite and the little girl is blamed as the carrier of ill-fortune. At puberty, in an intensely moving scene, her head is shaved and the colourful glass bangles she loves are ritually smashed. The lovely young girl's growing up, growing old and dying is portrayed with compassion, sensitivity and anger. In one memorable scene, she chances upon a young couple clandestinely making love and realises with devastation, that the only man to have ever touched her physically is the barber who comes once a month to shave her head. Her life, so filled with helping others has, in fact, been barren and empty, condemned to be so by formalized, man-made rules. At the end, she passes away as gently as she had lived, but not before supporting the spirited revolt of another 16-year-old widow who refuses to succumb to the same pattern. When this girl's husband dies, she thrusts her mother-in-law forward towards the appalled priests waiting to carry out the traditional mortifying practice of shaving her head and breaking her bangles. She marches off rebelliously — to pregnancy and marriage with her brother-in-law — leaving Phaniyamma to explain to the custodians of culture that "times have changed," and the dehumanisation of women so long sanctified can no longer be practised and will not be accepted.

Prema wrote the screenplay, based on a novel by M.K. Indira. She produced and directed *Phaniyamma* herself with a loan from the NFDC. Despite its prestige and success, it did not revive the embers of the flickering movement which had lasted just over a decade. However, in 1982, with Ramakrishna Hegde as Chief Minister, culture, particularly the cinema, was given a major boost. Subsidies to non-Kannada films were stopped, those for "art" films were raised substantially with incentives and encouragement, supplemented with cash prizes for State award-winning films. The chances of a revival are bright again.

In the meantime, some had abandoned film-making to return to writing, some had taken to teaching, others turned frankly commercial. A few had moved away, and the centre of the New Cinema had shifted further South, to Kerala, where a movement had been in the making for some time.

Kerala has the highest percentage of literacy (90%) in the country. It was the first state to vote the Communist Party to power in 1957. With its lush green landscape intersected by lakes, rivers and ocean inlets, its long sea coast and the last remaining rain forest in India, it escapes the urban-rural separation of the rest of the country. The capital, Trivandrum, is connected by a 228-mile-long navigable canal to Tirur in the north. Villages and small towns flow into each other. It has no single major city dominating the State either politically, geographically or culturally. Its matriarchal system, of which the remnants persist, is unique in India. Its only counterpart can be found in the North-East, among the Khasis of Meghalaya. It makes for a fascinating blend of culture and politics.

After Independence in 1947, the Communist Party of India (CPI) was quick to recognise the value of theatre in propagating the spread of ideas. The theatre-wing of the CPI, the Kerala Peoples' Artists Company took over where the Indian Peoples' Theatre Association, particularly active in Bengal in pre-Independence days, had left off. Film versions of their plays — *You Made me a Communist, Prodigal Son, New Sky, New Earth* were not quite as popular but they brought a number of theatre personalities into the cinema.

The close connection between theatre and cinema had certain disadvantages. Although films turned to Malayalam literature for the source of their screenplays, the technique remained stagey, with all films shot in studios.

Chemmeen in 1965 was one of the earliest to move out of the studios and into an actual location. Made by Ramu Kariat, it is a landmark in the development of Kerala cinema and gave him a national standing. Kariat was also an elected member of the Legislative Assembly in Kerala. By and large, however, the Malayali cinema was content to cater to popular taste, in imitation of its larger neighbour Tamil Nadu which had a flourishing film centre in its capital city, Madras.

In 1965, the year *Chemmeen* made history as the first film from the South to win the national best film award, Adoor Gopalakrishnan returned home to Trivandrum after graduating from the Film Institute at Pune. In those early days, nobody quite knew what the Film Institute stood for, neither the established industry nor even the Film Finance Corporation. In Kerala, says Adoor, "the whole industry laughed at you when you said you wanted to make a film. 'Classroom teaching doesn't work here, you have to have experience, you have to work in the field' they said. So in those days it was hard."*

But intense discussions about cinema, another kind of cinema, were possible with a cross section of people from other fields. Aravindan had met Adoor soon after he joined the Film Institute. His main interest then was in painting and he used to do regular cartoons for the literary magazine *Matrabhumi* whose young editor M.T. Vasudevan Nair was already a well-known novelist. Some of his writings had been adapted for films. All three also shared an interest in theatre. Adoor's interest in film grew out of the involvement with writing, directing and acting in plays. Aravindan today is well known as a director in the theatre as well as in the cinema. In the late fifties and early sixties, *Bicycle Thief, Bitter Rice, Rashomon* were among the films shown commercially in Trivandrum. Groups of artists and poets would gather in Aravindan's room to discuss what they had seen. Ghatak's films came as a revelation that "such films were being made in India also." They had seen and liked Bimal Roy and others but when they saw *Pather Panchali*, it was clear that "Satyajit Ray was something apart, speaking a whole new film language."*

However, the film industry was set in its ways, and had no time or place for other ideas in its scheme of things.

Adoor countered their scepticism by gathering other Institute graduates from different disciplines— camera, editing, sound— and together they set up the Chitralekha Film Cooperative, the first of its kind in India. They saw it as the start of a movement to build up new audiences and transform the approach to cinema through publishing film literature, starting film societies and taking on production, distribution and exhibition of what they considered "quality films". A manifesto of their aims was followed by the publication of the first film book in Malayalam with a collection of lectures and articles by Ghatak, Satyajit Ray, Balraj Sahni, *et al.* In the same year they formed the first Film Society. For the Films Division they managed to make a few documentaries, and applied to the FFC for a loan, which was turned down. The second time they came back to the FFC was for *Swayamvaram* (One's Own Choice), which Adoor made in 1972 as his first feature. M.T. Vasudevan Nair followed with *Nirmalayam* (Flower Offering) in 1973, and in 1974 Aravindan made *Uttarayanam* (Solstice). Kerala had arrived decisively on the national film scene.

In its choice of subjects as well as treatment, Kerala was entirely different from Karnataka. Brahminism, untouchability, the entire question of casteism, had been the principal preoccupation of the post-*Samskara* Kannada new cinema. In Kerala's somewhat different society, the issues were social and political, so that general problems emerged out of the dilemma of the individual. In Karnataka, the foreground was the community and a system that ensured the relative obscurity of the individual.

* Aravindan to the author.

Swayamvaram, told as a simple narrative, deals unsentimentally with the plight of an unmarried young couple, intensely in love. Fleeing parental disapproval, they arrive in a small town where the young man, carrying manuscripts of novels he has written, takes a temporary job in a college when he cannot find a publisher. When the college closes down, they exist precariously at the edge of poverty. Against a seedy environment their losing battle is waged. He dies, leaving her pregnant, alone and destitute. It is a bleak film with flashes of humanity in the compassion and concrete help extended by the couple's neighbours, who are hardly any better off. It passes no judgments, offers so solutions but on the contrary shows the beginning of an emerging middle class.

Adoor Gopalakrishnan's SWAYAMVARAM. 1972

Five years went by in building up the Cooperative, whose facilities now include camera and sound equipment, a laboratory, editing room, sound studios— everything necessary for making films. But Adoor has withdrawn from it and works independently, doing documentaries as well as feature films. *Kodiyettam* (The Ascent) 1977 was five years in the making. The equipment came from the Cooperative which produced it, but loans had to be raised "from friends". It shows the first signs of what Adoor would focus on more sharply in his next film *Elippathayam* (Rat Trap), 1981, about a man who is essentially a drifter, floating on the surface of the current, dependent on the women in his life, the last vestige of a matriarchal society. But while *Kodiyettam* shows the man finding himself and growing into a mature realisation of responsibility, *Elippathayam* has darker undertones and a denser structure. *Kodiyettam* is a gentle film full of poetic observations of characters and their settings. The man, played by Gopi, who was to become a nationally respected actor with a wide range and sensitivity, is an engaging layabout in a village, content to live off the earnings of his sister who works as a domestic servant in "the city". He is pampered by a childless widow and treated with amused tolerance by the people of the village. Marriage, which he enters into lightheartedly, hardly changes him. But slowly his world falls apart. His wife, disgusted with his irresponsible behaviour, returns home to her parents when she is pregnant. The sister starts living with her lover and can no longer support him. The widow commits suicide because of an unhappy affair with a married man (But it is her decision, not one she is forced into by stern social censure).

Adoor Gopalakrishnan's MUKHA MUKHAM, 1984

Bereft of all the warmth and protection he has so far enjoyed, he takes up a steady job and comes to terms with himself, his wife and his life.

By the time Adoor started on *Elippathayam,* he had sharpened his perceptions of cinema, without, as he says, being seduced by theories and abstractions. Individual characterisations are richer, the levels of experience deeper. In the picture of a decaying feudal family with its complex relationships, nuance and suggestion replace the more direct statements of *Swayamvaram* and *Kodiyettam.* To this he had added another, political dimension. Between the neurosis and rebelliousness implicit in the brother's refusal to face the changing socio-economic situation and the youngest sister's positive affirmation of it, lie layers of subtle insights into the passing of an old order and the adjustments, social, economic and psychological that had become necessary.

The switch to colour from the black-and-white of the earlier two films reveals Adoor's sophisticated aesthetic sense and the cameraman's (Madras Adyar Film Institute graduate Ravi Varma, on all Adoor's films) technical finesse. Velvet-black shadows and key lights, the brown wood of Kerala's old homes, dark flesh tones and white or coloured fabrics give all his films a sensuous texture. They have a distinctive style where the hand of the *auteur* is unmistakable. The sound track is sparer with each succeeding film until, with *Mukhamukham* (Face to Face), 1984, the main protagonist sinks into total silence. *Mukhamukham* unleashed a storm of controversy, disconcerting to the reserved, unostentatious director who in his ideas and about his work is nevertheless firm and confident. It was seen as a trenchant critique of the Communist Party in Kerala, arising from its failure to fulfil the hopes it had created. In fact, the film has a metaphysical dimension which goes beyond its immediate political surface. Adoor's commitment to the individual has not shifted. The apogee and the disarray of a contemporary movement which happens to be communism, forms a background to what is essentially a theme of the moral crisis of ordinary men and women, as much as *Elippathayam* has the decay of feudalism as the context against which individual lives are played out.

The most intricately constructed of Adoor's films, the deeper meaning in *Mukhamukham* is concealed beneath an apparently simple narrative scheme. Divided hardly perceptibly into two sections, the first part is a careful construction not of the man but an image of the man, the protagonist Shreedharan, as he appears to the people who talk about him. The second part is the destruction of that image at the same time as it is a "deconstruction" of it. Fiction and reality are ultimately indistinguishable.

In *Mukhamukham,* the first part of the film is "real", the second speculatory. The device Adoor uses to distinguish them is a visual and audial bracket. The second half is introduced with a scene where the old man, by the light of a single candle, reads out the *Bhagwatha* to his little grandson. The *Bhagwatha* is written in the form of a poem with the poet acting as a scribe, taking down the stories narrated by the holy parrot. "Tell us the rest of the story," the poet asks. "It is not easy," the bird answers. "Even for Guha and Ananda (who knew the secret of life) it was difficult. But I will try." With this the next part of the film begins. The transition is so imperceptible that it could be taken as a continuation of the earlier sequences. The electoral defeat of the CPI had driven many of its party cadres and workers underground. When it returned to power two years later (in 1957), many of them drifted back. Not Shreedharan. The family is told that he has died. Ten years have passed when the young son sits listening to his grandfather read from the *Bhagwatha.* Within the Party, dissatisfaction has set in; Shreedharan is a hero whose disappearance is still keenly felt. The same people who had created his image in the beginning *will* him back. When he does return, he has nothing to give them. Silent, alcoholic, he serves as a catalyst. The others, questioning, pleading, justifying, explaining, reveal their most private selves to him. As they realise he can help them no more than they can help themselves, his presence becomes unnecessary. The dream ends. To decipher all the metaphors, references, meanings and layers in this fascinating film requires a thorough acquaintance with not only India as a whole but Kerala in particular, its history, culture, philosophy, social behaviour and customs.

Barely suggested symbols, allusions to traditional practices in images or on the sound track enrich the already intricate weave of the film. The opening shot is highly evocative. A boat laden with clay glides down a sunlit river. "With these elements, earth, water, sun and air," the director seems to be saying, "I will create something." The confusion arises from Adoor's determination to make the dream appear as real as dreams sometimes do. As a result, the shift from reality into dream is so smooth and swift that it could be missed altogether. Seen as a narrative, it leaves many questions unanswered. It needs a stronger stylistic device for the attempt to be wholly successful. But there is no doubt that Adoor is working towards a kind of cinema quite unique in India. The development in form from the first film to the fourth is a testimony to his evolution as one of our foremost filmmakers today.

Twenty years earlier, Adoor was the first graduate in direction from the Film Institute to return to Kerala. The technicians who worked on his first film were also all trained at the Institute. *Swayamvaram* dominated the National Awards list, thrusting Adoor, the Film Institute and Kerala into the limelight. He was the first of the new breed of Institute graduates to win the Best Film award. A year later, when M.T. Vasudevan Nair, after seveal years of writing scripts for other peoples' films, decided to make his own, he chose Film Institute graduates to work on it. *Nirmalayam* uses superstition, trance, ritual, the temple as the focal point in a village, the new spirit of rationalism eroding practices held on to for centuries: it is a blend of many elements. The film ends in a crescendo with a trance-like dance in the village. It seemed to herald the arrival of another major talent, but M.T.'s later films did not live up to the potential clearly evident in *Nirmalayam*. He made three other films, two in Malayalam— *Varikuzzhi* and *Manju,* and one, *Sharad Sandhya,* in Hindi, but it seemed as if his heart was not in film making. He continues to write novels and short stories, while screenplays flow from his fertile pen with distinction. Perhaps that is his *forte,* his first and last love.

Both *Swayamvaram* and *Nirmalayam* together with the rapid expansion of film societies helped to create audiences for their kind of cinema. Aravindan had started the first film society in Kottayam in 1965 and then in Calicut. His fascination with cinema had been sparked off when he saw *Rashomon* and *Bitter Rice* in Trivandrum in the fifties— "a friend and I decided we wanted to study film making. So we wrote off to Hollywood knowing perfectly well we could not afford it."* Hollywood was, of course, the Mecca of film in those days. Europe was too distant, too much of an unknown entity. They never got a reply from Hollywood. It took several more years of seeing whatever they could manage on the commercial circuit and later on at the film societies before the idea and the possibility of making a film took shape.

A well-known writer friend with moneyed connections offered to raise the finances and, in 1974, Aravindan made *Uttarayanam,* in Hindu mythology the "good period". (Tagore's house in Shantiniketan is called Uttarayana). Before starting on it, he had everything planned, an unusual approach in those days. He was very clear that he wanted to make a realist film about a young man whose father is killed in the 1942 movement (for Independence). In its emphasis on realism, it shows little signs of the poetry that was to become the special characteristic of Aravindan's later films. It took another three years before he made *Kanchana Seeta* (Golden Sita) where the realism of the first film has vanished. For good, as his later work proved. Based on a well-known play by C.N. Sreekantan Nair, he chose for this film a tribe from Andhra Pradesh whose appearance struck him as ideal "to interpret, not act" the episode from the Hindu epic the Ramayana, upon which the play focusses. The tribals, called Ramachenchus, are considered descendants of Rama. But the play is only the source. In the film he never shows Sita, wife of the exiled king Rama. Represented as Parvati— all-pervading nature— her

* To the author

presence is felt everywhere, in the sighing of the breeze, the trembling of the leaves, the singing waters. It is visually breath-taking, poetically ambiguous. In the dark forest, pierced exquisitely by sudden rays of sunlight, the dark-skinned Rama wanders with his brother Lakshmana, intoxicated by memories of Sita whom he has been driven to abandon by an inexorable sense of duty. Aravindan's lyrically personal, contemplative style had been formed.

In *Thampe* (The Tent) 1978, he did choose an actor, Gopi, to play with actual performers in a poignant story about the lonely, transient life of a circus troupe, which becomes a metaphor for the lonely, transient nature of life itself.

Kummatty (The Bogeyman) shot in the same year as *Thampe,* was a fable for children, designed for a world of fantasy. *Esthappan* (Stephen) which followed in 1979 takes us back into Aravindan's mystical blending of poetry and ambiguity, touching upon the realm of the unknown and the inexplicable. He based *Kummatty* on the wandering story-tellers who go from village to village enchanting children like some Pied Piper of Hamelin. *Esthappan* is another such mysterious figure Aravindan says he has repeatedly encountered. Part saint, part prophet and healer, charlatan and quack, he eludes definition, living in the contradictory stories people weave around him. Beautifully shot in the earth colours of a Kerala fishing village where the sea is a living, breathing presence, it is a haunting film. The jarring note is struck by a group of young people (among whom is a European woman) who arrive in the village in a big boat. Their artificial gaiety and loud laughter at the house they rent is an irritating intrusion.

Aravindan's POKKUVEYIL, 1981

Perhaps Aravindan wanted them to serve as a reminder that the serenity of centuries was about to end, that new prosperity was bringing with it the vulgarity, the noise and the light of common day into a world where the imagination and the poetry of the unknown had held sway.

For five years Aravindan thought about the form he would adopt for *Pokkuveyil* (Twilight) before he eventually made it in 1981. The shape it took was that of a long lyric poem into whose texture are woven the broken dreams of love and politics and heroism. The main figure is that of a young poet. As he wanders along Kerala's peaceful backwaters dreaming his dreams, he encounters his friend, a revolutionary who tells him he has to go away and will call for him when the time comes. The poet, Balachandran, realises that dream is over. He stops for a while on the long empty line of the placid water with the girl he loves. She leaves for a bigger city with her parents. The basketball-player friend he admired so much for the physical grace he himself never possessed breaks a leg and is removed to a hospital, his power and his dream of becoming a pilot and flying free, trapped in a heavy, ugly plaster cast. The father Balachandran looked up to, dies. Like Shelley, he seems to say: "my brain grows dizzy; see'st thou shapes within the mist?" The film starts with his mother taking him to a mental asylum. It ends with her going to visit him there. The contemplative gaze of the film-maker is that of the poet by the seashore, who seems to become one with the sea, endlessly rolling, endlessly repeating its cycle. But it is not all part of a dreamer's vision. The poems recited are those written by the young man, a well-known poet in Kerala who appears as himself in the film. Stunning visual images, a sound track

Aravindan's CHIDAMBARAM. 1985

in which the murmur of the sea merges with the (North Indian) classical music and the voice of the poet, give the film a hypnotic quality.

So far, Aravindan has remained true to himself. Not interested in film theories, he says that style is dictated by the content, and he shapes his films on the editing table. He prefers to work with non-professional actors because "film is definitely a director's medium. And for my type of film any reasonably intelligent person will do because what is required is behaviour, not acting." The persona of the actor, in other words, must not be allowed to interfere with the director's vision. But, for his seventh film *Chidambaram,* he took Smita Patil and, once again, Gopi, both of them professional actors with strong personalities. While Gopi is able to transcend his own self to recreate the character of Sankaran in the film, Smita Patil's Sivakami is less successful. However, the film belongs to Sankaran, another haunting incarnation of Aravindan's solitary, mysterious wanderer.

It is as close to narrative as Aravindan is likely to get, yet it is his most enigmatic film. His refusal to be explicit borders on unintelligibility yet each scene pulses with meaning. Visual and aural understatement, Aravindan's chosen style, are carried to extremes in this film. A sensuous perception of culture and custom and tradition, philosophy and religion, impose the burden of understanding on the viewer. It is not enough, for instance, to grasp the literal meaning of the words of the songs. One has also to know the context, the why and when and by whom they were first composed and sung, in order to realise the significance of their use in the film. In Sankaran's flight to Chidambaram we have to know not only that this is Sivakami's home town but that the temple of Chidambaram is where the great god Siva manifested himself as the cosmic dancer. Here that Nandanar, the Harijan saint whose songs Muniyandi (Sivakami's husband) sings to Sankaran in the beginning, sang his songs in praise of Siva and the doors of the temple were miraculously opened to allow him a glimpse of the image of the deity. And it is here that Sankaran finds ultimate release from physical desire and guilt as the camera moves up the temple *gopuram* and into the sky.

The old woman he saw, was she Sivakami transformed? Or a vision, a waking dream? Had Muniyandi killed her, his wife, before killing himself, broken by Sankaran's betrayal of his trust? It is of no consequence. Aravindan prefers the poetry of conjecture to the unequivocal fact. It is the colours that suggest mood and ideas. Aravindan uses colour as a philosopher might. Sensual, fertile greens dissolve into dusty greys, and browns as cracked and bleak as Sankaran's soul, until release comes with the ineffable blue of the sky. The journey is ended, the torment over. Aravindan leaves one alone with the religious and philosophical implications of the experience we have been through.

The work of these three directors stimulated an enthusiastic interest in the cinema within Kerala. "In the sixties the talk at University campuses was of literature. Today it is cinema," says Adoor Gopalakrishnan. With over a hundred film societies in a State with a population of 11 million, there are enough audiences to make even "difficult" films financially viable. Producers and financiers are prepared to back such films for the prestige and awards they bring, particularly when the budgets are reasonable and the risk of losing money is minimal. Today in Kerala, it is said, people are either watching films or making them.

In 1984, Ravi Varma directed a film himself. In *Nokkukuthi* (The Bugaboo) traditional bards chant a legend, a love story that ends in terrible tragedy as the members of a powerful Brahmin clan behead the lower-caste girl one of their own has dared to marry. Defiance of codes shall not be tolerated even if murder has to be done to preserve them! Seen through the contemporary eyes of a young couple, it is exquisitely shot, as one might well expect from Varma, Adoor Gopalakrishnan's cameraman. But it remains a cameraman's film. The other elements of pace, editing, rhythm, structure, do not live up to the beauty of its visual images. The attempt, once again, has a certain interest, with chanting and singing entirely replacing dialogue.

Other Film Institute graduates have followed in Adoor's footsteps. Among them K.G. George is the most prolific and the most interesting. Starting with *Swapnadanam* (Journey through a Dream) in 1975, he has made about one film a year. Many of his films take up the theme of the exploitation of women. In *Lekhayude Maranam Oru Flashback* (Lekha's Story) 1983, he exposes the manner in which women are degraded and, sometimes, driven to suicide in the film world. Based on the true story of a young actress, it was bitterly attacked by the film industry for its "distortions". *Yavanika* (The Curtain) 1982 is a psychological exploration of character, set in the background of a Touring Theatre Group in Kerala. The violent conflict engendered by the closeness and claustrophobia of their lives is treated in the form of a cleverly constructed mystery thriller. *Adaminte Variyellu* (Adam's Rib), 1984, is the most severe attack yet on the treatment of women. Three separate stories, three different women, lay bare different facets of the same tyranny.

The critical and commercial success of these films led others to turn from painting, writing

Gopi in K.G. George's YAVANIKA. 1982

and theatre to cinema. B.G. Bharathan, painter and sculptor, began working in films as an art director and publicity designer before becoming a film director. Love, marriage and contemporary society form the nucleus of his concerns. P. Padmarajan, well-known in Kerala as a short story writer and novelist entered films by way of script writing, including some for Bharathan. In their late thirties, they share the view that the narrative is the important part of

J. Mahendran's NENJATHAI KILLATHE. 1980

Biplab Roy Chowdhury's SHODH. 1979

film making. A good story, a strong screenplay, are what matters. It is an attitude that is the basis for the rise of a "middle" cinema in almost all the Indian languages, including Hindi, treading gingerly between the two extremes of "art" and "commerce". K.S. Sethumadhavan, a fairly conservative director, came out with *Oppol* (Elder Sister) in 1980. Written by M.T. Vasudevan Nair, it has the courage to go against traditional values in showing the strong bond between an unmarried woman and her child.

It might have been expected that the tide of the "New Wave" would flow into the two other Southern States of Tamil Nadu and Andhra Pradesh. But at best it is only a lapping at the shores.

In Tamil Nadu the cinema for decades had a unique relationship with politics. Politically-aware script-writers and directors began using cinema as a forum for the expression of political views as far back as the fifties. Actors were drawn into the fray, and became identified with opposing parties. In 1949 C.N. Annadurai, a popular and powerful screenplay writer, formed a new party, the DMK (Dravidian Progressive Movement), and in 1967 this party was voted into power in the state of Tamil Nadu with Annadurai as Chief Minister.

For the eighteen years since then, the political scene in Tamil Nadu has been dominated by writers or actors, by the DMK or the breakaway party, the Anna DMK formed by M.G. Ramachandran, the superstar, who has been Chief Minister since 1977. With the emphasis on writers, the tendency in the Tamil cinema was to place an excessive stress on verbalisation. K. Balachander brought a more visual sense to his cinema, tackling middle-class issues in a realist vein in marked contrast to the overblown rhetoric of the popular cinema. Bharathi Raja though working within the commercial framework, moved the Tamil cinema out of the studios and into village locales. J. Mahendran with a background in theatre and journalism (an editor of the satirical periodical *Tughlak*) continued the pattern of the middle-of-the-road cinema emerging everywhere as an alternate genre. His *Nenjathai Killathe* (Don't Pinch the Heart), 1980, shows the steady growth of his sensibility and craft since his first *Mullum Malarum* (A Thorn and a Flower) in 1978. The arrival of technicians trained at the Pune Institute as well as the Adyar Film Institute in Madras was in large measure responsible for the different cinematic approach that ushered in the seventies. Balu Mahendra, another Pune-trained cameraman took to direction and produced a string of pleasantly watchable films. The themes may not be startling or the form exciting but he brings to his work a feel and care for craftsmanship, in itself refreshing.

John Abraham, originally from Kerala, had in fact been at University with Aravindan, before going to live in Madras. A Pune Film Institute graduate*, he had worked as Mani Kaul's assistant on *Uski Roti*. In 1977 he made *Agraharthil Kazhuthai* (Donkey in a Brahmin Village). He denies firmly that he was affected by Bresson's *Au Hasard Balthazar,* saying that he only saw it after he had completed his own film! However, the structure and pace of *Agraharthil* are clearly marked by European, particularly French influences, and in his approach to cinema his affinities lie with Mani Kaul and Kumar Shahani. It is a whimsical satire on the obscurantism, bigotry and hypocrisy of Brahmin priests as they blame the little donkey for every single thing that goes wrong in the village. They have it killed, and then fall a prey to the superstitious belief that by doing so they have brought a curse on themselves. To the utter bewilderment of the University professor who had adopted the little donkey and then, ordered by the principal (a Christian priest) to get rid of it, had taken it to his village, the Brahmin priests end by building a temple to it. It is the manner in which Abraham structures the story that its strength as cinema lies; the narrative is broken up by direct comment and asides which appear tangential but are never irrelevant. Abraham's reputation rests on *Agraharthil Kazhuthai* which he made with

* ("I pin my hopes on Kumar Shahani, John Abraham...." Ghatak had said)

private, family financing. It had no audience in Tamil Nadu, but was extensively seen at special screenings and film societies in Kerala and where it was also released briefly on the commercial circuit. Abraham's weakness is alcohol, which had a disastrous effect on the next film he made in Malayalam *Cheriyachante Kroora Krithyangal* (The Wicked Deeds of Cheriyachan. It had all the makings of an extraordinary work which never quite came off. He is now working on another.

Another Institute graduate is K. Hariharan. Emerging from the security of the Institute was often a traumatic experience for its young students. They tended to stick close to each other or gather round earlier graduates. In Bombay, Mani Kaul together with Hariharan, Saeed Mirza and others, set up the Yukt Film Cooperative. Their first venture was *Ghasiram Kotwal,* made in Marathi in 1977. A play by Vijay Tendulkar, it had been frequently and very successfully staged by Jabbar Patel and the Pune-based Theatre Academy, some of whose members also acted in the film. Financial problems and lack of distribution outlets inhibited the Cooperative from further efforts. Hariharan returned to Madras and made a few documentaries before finally raising private funds for his *Ezhavathu Manithan* (Seventh Man) in Tamil, completed in 1982. In its labour-management confrontation, it has a strong subject. Underlying the clash which is the central core of the story is the implication that new relations of production were breaking down class differences even in rural societies. The film has a certain validity but the absence of formal values is surprising in someone with Hariharan's background.

A director who derived a comprehensive education from contemporary world cinema without going to the Film Institute is Shreedhar Rajan. Living a cosmopolitan life working with a publishing house in Delhi, far removed from his native Tamil in culture and language, Shreedhar was, as he says, shaken by his encounter with Latin American, particularly Cuban cinema at the International Film Festival in 1977. He had long discussions with Umberto Solas, studied and wrote about the films he saw. It was a turning point in his life. He went back to his home town Madras, and immersed himself in the study of Tamil— the culture and the language— with a view to making films himself. Somendhu Roy (Satyajit Ray's cameraman in his later films) came from Calcutta to shoot it. *Kann Sivanthaql Man Sivakkum* (Hangmen's Hymns) 1982 is the first line of a poem by the great Tamil poet Subramania Bharathi, whose poems were also used by John Abraham in *Agraharthil Kazhuthai* and by K. Hariharan in *Ezhavathu Manithan.*

Shreedhar Rajan tries to encompass so many ideas into his film, it is almost as if he felt he would never make another and therefore had to say it all at once. But one can feel his excitement with ideas in the abstract as also in the discovery of living traditions from which he, like so many intellectual, urban, Anglicized Indians were and still are, cut off. In the film, two such young people, an artist with revolution on his mind, and a Bharatanatyam dancer who returns to India from "abroad" literally in search of roots, travel together into the heart of Tamil Nadu to seek out Thambiram, an ageing exponent of the dying dance form Theru-Koothu, from which Bharatanatyam is thought to have evolved. The story that is interpreted in the dance is of the tenth century Harijan Saint Nandanar, whose devout worship of the god Siva is said to have opened the temple doors to him despite the opposition of the Brahmins. The story of Nandanar becomes a metaphor for contemporary reality, as the two young people are confronted with actual events and characters in the village, and experience the fear and the oppression still continuing centuries after the death of Nandanar. The film has a dense structure but suffers from a lack of control and craftsmanship. If Shreedhar Rajan could acquire the rigour this kind of film-making demands, he could emerge as one of the most exciting new film-makers. He has the potential. He needs the polish.

In Andhra Pradesh, the politics-cinema connection in the neighbouring state of Tamil Nadu produced a similar result with N.T. Rama Rao, long-time star of hundreds of mythological

—K. Hariharan's EZAVATHU MANITHAN. 1982

films, forming a political party, Telugu Desam, and winning the elections to become Chief Minister in 1983. Andhra Pradesh has a well-entrenched and highly popular cinema in its own language Telugu. In 1977, Mrinal Sen was invited by a producer from this State to make a film in Telugu. Mrinal, always ready to meet a challenge, produced *Oka Oorie Katha* in 1977.* The same year Shyam Benegal went to Andhra which is his home state and where he had already shot *Ankur* and *Nishant,* to shoot *Anugraham* in Telugu (*Kondura* in the Hindi version)**. Two years later, Goutam Ghose was asked by B. Narsing Rao and G. Ravindranath to come and shoot *Ma Bhoomi* in Telengana, the area of Andhra Pradesh where the Telengana movement had its origins.***

These three films did not have immediate and obvious repercussions on the Telugu film industry. But Narsing Rao, a painter with private means and definite sympathy for the revolutionary movements of Telengana and Naxalbari, directed his own film in 1984, *Rangula Kala.* It is the eternal conflict of the artist with his social conscience. Playing the main role himself, he watches one friend climb the ladder of artistic and financial success through clever promotion; he listens to another who argues that art which does not assist the masses in their struggle for survival has no relevance and no validity. It underlines the dilemma of the artist in India today, without making any moral judgements. It is beautifully shot by Venugopal K.

* See page 30
** See page 40-4
*** See pages 67-68

Thakker. In theme and craftsmanship, it is in line with the middle cinema attracting film makers all over the country.

B.S. Narayana has been working in a similar genre since 1960. His *Nimajjanam* (The Immersion), 1979, examines with care and sensitivity the trauma of rape and the utter helplessness of the woman. A criticism of rigid Brahminic customs, muted and understated is the sub-text of the film.

With so few films to challenge its hold on the public imagination, the popular cinema in Andhra Pradesh has little to fear and no incentive to shift from its accepted norms.

9

FORM AND FUNCTION

The immediate reaction to Mani Kaul's *Uski Roti* in 1970, was one of shock. And in the fifteen years since then, the reaction has changed only marginally. *Sara Akash,* even *Bhuvan Shome* and *Ankur* soon after, brought a linear dramatic structure to the Indian cinema— in itself something new in its time and context. The humanist school had gained sanction and acceptance through Satyajit Ray. *Pather Panchali* was a turning point in a number of ways. *Uski Roti* was another pivotal moment. Mani Kaul spurned realism as a style. His style derives indirectly from the teaching and work of Ritwik Ghatak, and from a strain of contemporary European cinema. But in *Uski Roti* and even more in his subsequent films, Mani Kaul never falls into the trap of mere imitation. It is a singular idiom he created, neither imitative nor imitable. The influences are never evident because they have been thoroughly internalised, as with Kumar Shahani. "My intellectual awareness is my equipment," he has said. Although he admires Tarkovsky and Bresson and Ozu immensely, the man responsible for the "more or less physical transformation I went through was Ritwik Ghatak," says Kaul. That "physical transformation" was combined with deep introspection and an intellectual inquiry into the nature of cinema, the meaning of tradition and the sensuousness that gives it vibrancy, the parasitic relationship of cinema with the other arts, the determination to destroy it in order to construct "a purely cinematic object" and, while maintaining continuity with one kind of tradition of cinema, arrive at a new consciousness.

It was something few of the progressive film makers had understood that although the thematic content of their films may be liberal, advanced, forward-looking, the real relations with people or their world attitude revealed a sensuousness, a way of relating to ideas, people and life itself, which was still very old. "For me an artistic activity is one that somehow attempts to alter this sensuousness," Mani Kaul says. And this, in his work, is extended to the materials of cinema itself, beyond the filmic image into theatre, literature and painting, which the cinema has always fed upon. "Cinema for me is a plastic, not a performing art," he says. "It should be direct sculpting in time."*

From his first film *Uski Roti,* Kaul discards plot and narrative, to reach beyond communicating information into seeking a new relationship with the person looking at his film. Obsessed with the idea that there should be no trace of theatre, therefore no psychology of

* Interview, in *Indian Cinema Superbazaar, op cit.* pp 232-242

— Mani Kaul's SATAH SE UPTHATA ADMI. 1980

characters, he drains the acting and the situations of all vestiges of drama. *Uski Roti* is based on a short story by Mohan Rakesh. Kaul does not flesh it out, expand it in time to suit the length of a feature film. The pace is slow, unrelenting, with a rigorous rhythm of its own. The images are stark; they hold in them the distilled essence of sorrow and solitude. Silences enfold you, force you to face yourself. There is no escape.

Ashad Ka Ek Din (A Monsoon Day), 1971, takes as a starting point a play by the same writer, Mohan Rakesh. It is another step in Mani Kaul's exploration of the intimacy between the Word and the Cinema. From the short story to a play, and the cinema begins to free itself of bondage to words and scripts, to use a text without distorting either literature or cinema. The monotones of the actors, the heavy, stylized movements robbed equally of drama and of realism make one intensely, physically aware of the timbre of voices, of textures, of light, of what cinema is capable of accomplishing. What Kaul was striving towards in *Ashad Ka Ek Din,* seems effortlessly attained in *Satah Se Uthata Admi* (Arising from the Surface) in 1980. Here he dispenses with a conventional film script altogether while using the text of the writings— stories, poems, essays— of Gajanan Madhav Muktibodh, improvising with both cinema and text in much the same way as classical Indian music is improvised on a determined scale. The struggle seen in *Ashad Ka Ek Din,* soars with a stern lyricism in the later film. Through images and texts, not fused but made distinct, we see into the mind of Muktibodh and into the manner in which Mani Kaul sees into Muktibodh's mind. It is brilliantly conceived and brilliantly finished. The inflexibility which sometimes came through in the earlier films has vanished, to be replaced by grace and suppleness. The "obsession that there should be no trace of theatre" has given way to the confident knowledge that no trace does remain, releasing Kaul's cinema from all constraints in a final severing of the bonds.

Montage, building up scenes through relating different fragments to each other, close-ups, cutaways, details, do not form a part of Kaul's film language. Each shot is treated as a whole, complete in itself. The shelving of plot and drama was taking him into an area which is close to a highly original form of documentary. From literature to music: in *Drupad* (a style/school of classical singing) he sees, and makes us see, the similarity between music and architecture in the organisation of volume and space. In *Satah Se Uthata Admi* he had, through Muktibodh's writings, hinted visually at the conflict between the idealist and the material world, between labour and capital. *Dhrupad* closes with a five-minute shot over the roofscape of Bombay. The beauty and organisation of the music trying to find some sense in the city's anarchic, chaotic spread?

Between *Ashad Ka Ek Din* and *Satah Se Uthata Admi* Kaul had returned to Rajasthan where, born in a Kashmiri family, he had grown up. For *Duvidha* (In Two Minds), 1973, he took a folk tale and used colour for the first time, but colour which, in its visual scale, recalls black and white: brilliant reds and yellows against dazzling white. For the only time he has a story to tell. At the same time it is an analysis of myths and how they operate, become sensuous.

Uski Roti, Ashad Ka Ek Din and *Duvidha* were all financed by the FFC, and *Satah Se Uthata Admi* by the Government of Madhya Pradesh. The Film Finance Corporation in those early years was waging a lonely and not always easy battle as an institution prepared to assist such non-conformist ideas against tremendous odds. The Government had created it as a promotional body where return on investment, the purpose of a commercial financing institution, was not the mandate. B.K. Karanjia, its honorary chairman, had to fight hard to support a cinema ahead of its time.

Kumar Shahani and Mani Kaul had been colleagues and friends at the FTII. Formed by the same master Ritwik Ghatak, their perceptions of cinema honed by the same sensibility, their work takes different directions, yet they are invariably mentioned in the same breath. On graduating from the Institute, **Kumar** received a French Government scholarship to spend a year in France. He attended classes at the Institut des Hautes Etudes Cinematographiques, but the most significant aspect of his year in Paris was the intimate exposure to Robert Bresson on whose *Une Femme Douce* he was a *stagiaire* (apprentice). It was not a coincidence but a conscious decision on Shahani's part. Bresson's cinema possessed the qualities Shahani wished to work towards— "In Paris I saw *Au Hasard Balthazar*. It is really beautiful, like music, like a melody. I decided that I was going to work with him if I could possibly manage it." As much as the musicality that Shahani admired, Bresson works within a classical European tradition. From Ghatak and the historian D.D. Kosambi, Shahani had learnt and then developed his own ideas on the meaning of tradition and the epic form. Through the invaluable association with Bresson he was able to advance and elaborate those ideas when he returned home.

India with its many levels and layers, its inbuilt contradictions, its pulsating images and rhythms was both unnerving and invigorating. For the Indian artist, "the problem of relating to his contemporary world has been the most important challenge. To meet this challenge without ready-made answers, without sloganmongering, has been specifically the problem of the radical artist."* For Kumar Shahani the problem was most acute. To relate to the contemporary world involved making a political statement, yet realism, with its capacity to evoke emotional responses without forcing the viewer into a position of having to make decisions, was not the answer for him. Sensuousness plus the maintaining of a distance essential for rational thought; the need to make images and sounds significant in themselves, to mould and bend and reshape cinema to meet these challenges, was what engaged him. For his first film *Maya Darpan* (The Mirror of Illusion) 1972, he worked out the details of the design, form and style through the use of colour.

Based on a story by the respected contemporary Hindi writer Nirmal Verma, *Maya Darpan* portrays the oppression and the isolation of feudalism— social and personal— in a society moving inexorably into industrialisation. The long tracking shots at the beginning of the film establish the rhythm, the ambience and Shahani's approach. The young woman Taran lives in an old, decaying, colonial house whose high ceilings and colonnaded corridors recall Imperial splendour, her only companions her silent, brooding father and an elderly widowed aunt. Her mother is long dead, her only brother working at a tea estate in Assam. Beyond the grounds of the house the world is changing as machines ravage the earth in a determination to subdue nature and harness its strength in the service of man. The red bricks, the brown dry earth, the palpable heat, reduce Taran to a state of somnambulism in which she dreams of escape into the cool, green hills of Assam's tea estates. Echoes of the changing environment in the world outside reach Taran, awakening her by hardly perceptible degrees to the possibility of change within herself. Attracted to the young engineer from the city who is supervising the construction of the factory, she goes to him of her own volition. "Freedom," Shahani quotes Friedrich Engels in his film, "is the recognition of necessity." Once Taran recognises that her father's oppression and helplessness are equally involuntary, she is free to be "fierce and tender, objectively." She rejects the dream of living in Assam. She decides to stay where she is, identifying within herself both the terrible and the nurturing aspects of the mother-goddess. This realization is introduced visually by a single brief shot of her nude, painted blue, a clear reference to the Indian mother-goddess.

Colour is used with deliberation. The red-to-green tonal movement in the film and the harshness of the light in an arid landscape are perfectly orchestrated, inducing moods and images. Red and black are used to evoke Kali, the terrifying goddess worshipped as mother,

* Interview in *Indian Cinema Superbazaar,* op cit p. 275

* Arun Khopkar — "The works of Mani Kaul and Kumar Shahani" in *70 years of Indian Cinema,* ed T.M. Ramachandran. Cinema-India International, Bombay 1985.

creator and destroyer. The reds and yellows of the earlier part indicate the suppressed violence that is within Taran as it is in her environment. Green suggests the lushness of Assam in Taran's longings for release, the inner quietude she achieves in the latter part of the film. The end comes in red, black and white— "the primary colours of fertility, as her sexual encounter with the engineer opens out into the Chhau dance."* The camera and the dancers move together, the camera craning down repeatedly, the dancers moving up and out of the top of the frame, expressing a sense of ineffable release.

The final shot is of serene green hills and quiet lakes. From fire to water. Passion and procreation. An assertion of life.

Seeing *Maya Darpan,* Mansell Stimpson wrote in *Film* (London 1973) "If other directors are copying avant-garde techniques from the West, Shahani alone displays the originality of genius." And Louis Marcorelles, writing in *Le Monde* nine years later: *"Maya Darpan* is a work of great beauty.... obviously Marxist, with a certain loftiness. Shahani does not copy anyone. He makes colour work for him; he captures spaces, makes you actually feel the weight of objects, fabrics, light itself."

It was twelve years before Shahani came out with another film, *Tarang* (The Wave). Twelve years to sharpen his ideas still further, twelve years in which he made a few documentaries, lectured at the Film Institute, universities and film societies, studied the epic form on a two-year fellowship.

Tarang was started in 1978 with a loan from the NFDC, but the producer backing it obviously felt it was not going to be the commercial film he had imagined from the script, and abandoned it. Ultimately rescued by the NFDC, it was completed in 1984.

In its three hours, Shahani explores the wealthy, industrial face of India, the bourgeoisie that has emerged since Independence, its relations with the labour force swayed by Marxist thinking, the clash between expatriate Indians in league with the multi-nationals and the fierce nationalists proud of indigenous achievements but unable to shake off centuries of class differences and the remnants of feudal, exploitative attitudes. Within, not against, this vast context, the personal lives of individuals have their being, and their end. The conflict between two branches of the family which brings destruction in its wake has something of the spirit of the Mahabharata where everyone is treating with equal respect. In the epic tradition a similar imagery may be used for types," with each character individuated through other means. *Tarang* works within such a tradition. It is entirely contemporary, encompassing in its amplitude the flow of ideas and events that have swept India in the decades since Independence. It is far removed from the realism that must have a central plot and drama. It is a narrative in the sense that the epic is narrative. Shahani does not allow the spectator to be "in the thick of it, sharing the experience." Instead, a distance is maintained whereby you are always standing outside, an observer forced into taking decisions, alterable and able to alter."* But as always with Shahani, the reference is never obvious. The knowledge and the influence are thoroughly internalised to emerge in a uniquely original form. We watch, we are not swept into, the events and characters as they unfold with an inevitability which transcends the individual tragic flaw.

The complex structure of *Tarang* demands a large number of characters. At the centre is Shethji (Shriram Lagoo), the patriarch of an industrial empire living in Bombay with his daughter Hansa (Kawal Gandhiok- in her first film appearance), her husband Rahul (Amol Palekar) and their small son. A nephew Dinesh (Girish Karnad) lives in London and appears briefly in Bombay but his presence is felt throughout the film. The presence of Khala (Abdul's mother) is similarly felt although she actually appears in barely three scenes. Outside the family

* Ashish Rajadhyaksha *Ritwik Ghatak, A Return to the Epic.* Screen Unit, Bombay 1982 pp. 139-140

* Bertolt Brecht: *Brecht on Theatre, The Development of an Aesthetic.* Radhakrishna Prakashan, Delhi 1979, p. 37.

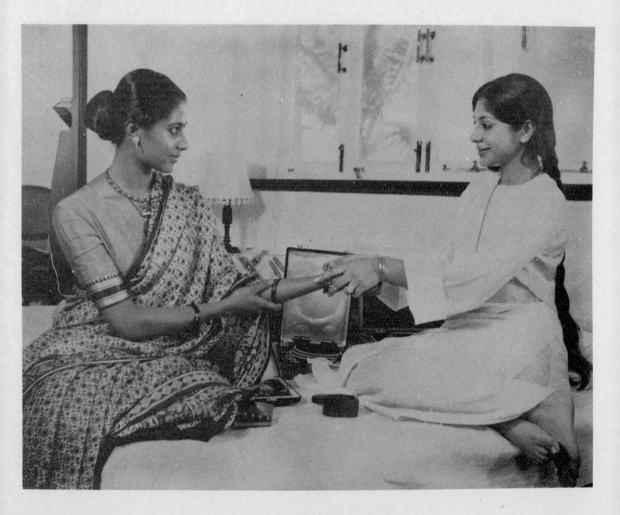

Kumar Shahani's TARANG, 1984

living in their luxurious house by the sea, is the world of the factory workers. Connecting the two is the corrupt trade-union leader Patel, and Janaki (Smita Patil). As the wife of a factory worker who was killed accidentally, she is trusted and respected by the workers, among whom are her friends Abdul (M.K. Raina) and Namdev (Om Puri). Thrown out of her shack by the police at Shethji's instigation, she is forced to walk the streets until Rahul employs her to look after his little boy. Gradually, almost imperceptibly, the archetype of the mother-goddess emerges in her. From the workers, to the man who picks her up in the street and weeps on her shoulder, to Rahul's little son, to Hansa herself, she is the nurturing mother-figure. Tender and loving, she can also be the destroyer as she follows Rahul's unspoken wish and conspires to let the old man die. Hansa, wrapped up in her father, the only man she really loves, understands that a relationship is developing between Rahul and Janaki. She tacitly acquiesces in it. Between Janaki and Hansa an indefinable bond grows as Hansa encourages Janaki to try on her jewellery, her clothes, her role as wife and mother in the house. Conflict intensifies between Dinesh, who wants Shethji to collaborate with a multi-national company and Rahul who believes in indigenisation and workers' rights to higher wages provided they lead to higher productivity. He would prefer to deal with the professional Communist trade-union leader rather than with the corrupt Patel who would betray both Shethji and the workers if it were to his personal advantage. Rahul's own motivations are ambiguous. The outward appearance of the dynamic, liberal, modern Indian masks a driving ambition. With Shethji out of the way, he wins the loyalty of the old man's confidential secretary (Rohini Hattangady) with whom he has had an affair, getting her married to a friend of his (Jalal Agha). Among the workers, trouble is fomented by the crooked trade-union leader, an ally of Dinesh. Communal passions are engineered, and culminate in violence. Abdul has to go into hiding. Rahul manipulates the situation to his own advantage.

Hansa, filled with sorrow at her father's death, believing it was Rahul's refusal to negotiate with Dinesh that caused it, withdraws from life itself. Moving listlessly through the house, she resembles Taran in *Maya Darpan*. In one beautiful sequence, she walks through the forest bathed in a sensuous light. On the soundtrack is a song expressing the thoughts in her mind. It is the commercial cinema's technique brilliantly inverted and made significant rather than used as a convenient device. Hansa dies in water, flowers strewn around her. The reference to Ophelia and Hamlet is unmistakable.

Rahul, free now, he imagines, to indulge his ambitions, is suspected by Dinesh of having arranged Shethji's death. Fear brings out his latent feudal arrogance. He seeks out Janaki in the hills where he had sent her with the little boy, tells her she will have to bear the guilt if the suspicion against him turns into an accusation. Janaki is stunned at this betrayal. She leaves immediately. Alone again, she walks down the long, curving hill road. Rounding bend after bend the trucks roar up, seeming to encircle and enfold her.

Janaki finds Namdev, a temporary refuge. Tensions flare up around them. The workers' shacks are set on fire. Rahul, terrified at the disintegration of what he had intrigued for and conspired to win and to hold, looks again for Janaki— the nurturing motherfigure who can save him from the fruits of his own cowardice. On a long empty bridge across an expanse of still water, as the first of the sun's rays appear, he sees her, and pleads with her to return. But she has become Usha, goddess of the dawn, and she tells him, "I have passed away like the first of the dawns... I am like the wind, difficult to catch."

Through this rich, demanding, rewarding film Shahani, like Jean-Marie Straub with whom he has been compared, seems to be attempting a deconstruction of conventions, refusing to satisfy the expectations people bring to the cinema, and by that very refusal increasing awareness of them. It is a disturbing, uncomfortable process he is engaged in, where conventions of cinema and perceptions of characters and relationships are equally challenged. In Hansa, for example, unthinkingly accepted notions of the relations between wife and husband, daughter and father, man and mistress, are tested. The revolutionary Namdev becomes a Christ-like figure. Stereotypes are demolished, the significant set free.

Power is central to the theme of *Tarang,* its use and misuse as it passes from Shethji to Rahul to Janaki on one plane. The police, the workers, the union leaders, jockey for it on another, using all possible means to acquire and exercise it themselves. Only the strangely mysterious Hansa, wrapped up in a world of her own, remains unconcerned, outside the struggle.

The acting style shifts between the lyrical and the stylised, from subjectivity to objectivity and back again. "The method of the acting evolved from *Mayà Darpan* to meet the demands of the epic. I think the actor's own being should never be denied if you wish to discover the archetype," Kumar Shahani says.* He also subscribes to the Bazinian ideal of *mise-en-scene.* There are no quick cuts, no collision of opposites, nor do gestures signal the end of the shot as in the classic Hollywood norm. Movements take place within the shot itself as an inner rhythm dictates the editing pattern. The majesty of Vanraj Bhatia's music, using Western instrumentation to improvise on Indian *ragas* enhances or counterpoints the harmony as well as the clash of characters and cultures.

The film is shot in Cinemascope which, writes Arun Khopkar, "allows deployment of visual forces along the lines of a triptych. Depth of field is not used for a continuous, infinite focus but along well-defined planes. The lighting and colour sometimes alter the physical relationship between the planes. The cranes, the straight and the circular trolley are used to maintain a dynamic point of view which is not reducible to dramatic significance alone."**

Kumar Shahani's formidable intellect will not allow him to make the slightest concessions. "The artist does more than he knows," it has been said. But Shahani always knows what he is doing. That it might remove an element of spontaneity from his work he also recognises. "I do not agree with the idea of improvisation which has developed over the last twenty years. I would rather take the classicist form of improvisation — that you have the structure to start with and shade it as you go along, perhaps even coming to a point where you destroy that structure internally."* He is currently in the process of making a film on the life and work of the psycho-analyst Wilfrid Bion who was born in India at the turn of the century.

The instinct for knowledge, a concern with archetypes, mythology and dreams, forms the basis of Bion's psychoanalytical work in which "he has tried to find neutral symbols for the creation of a theory of emotions, symbols devoid of associative, moralistic or other forms of loaded concepts." His fictional works show "a grasp of extra-rational reality (which) goes deep into the mystical traditions of the East,"** Shahani says, who has visualised the film as a fantasy.

In the sequences shot so far, dream and reality, past and present, fuse and scatter in startlingly evocative images and patterns. Its international cast — Nicholas Clay, Peter Firth, Carol Drinkwater, Angela Pleasance joining Alaknanda Samarth, Tom Alter and Jalal Agha, with location shooting required in India, France and England, demand a large budget and complicated production problems. The initial financing came from the Psychoanalytic Trust in England. Further work has been unfortunately held up pending the availability of funds.

Mani Kaul and Kumar Shahani are Ritwik Ghatak's most illustrious disciples. About Shahani, Ghatak had said, "Kumar Shahani is my best student. When he comes out with his

* Interview with Rajiv Rao and Rafique Baghdadi in *The Sunday Observer,* Bombay 29 April, 1984
** Arun Khopkar, *op cit.*

* "Interview with Madan Gopal Singh": *Festival News No. 4,* January 1985; ed. Aruna Vasudev, Cendit and Directorate of Film Festivals, New Delhi.
** Interview with Rajiv Rao and Rafiq Baghdadi, *op cit.*

films, it will be staggering."* On the surface there is no similarity in the work of all three, but "Ghatak never expected or wanted us to imitate him," Shahani says. His ideas, his approach, his understanding, were assimilated and internalized by his students in a manner that helped them to develop their own personal, individual styles.

A handful of other film makers, Kaul's and Shahani's successors at the Film Institute in Pune, are working in a similarly creative vein, where form, acting, music, camera, lighting, structure, the materials of cinema are used in ways designed to alter the perceptions of cinema and awaken a new consciousness. They understand style to be as ideologically determined as the text; their attempt is to operate at a deeper level of cultural production. To them as to Shahani even more than Kaul, cinema is an art through which contemporary reality is refracted. Their respect and love for the cinema will not permit them to use it as an obvious "weapon", a carrier of radical messages by means of which large audiences can be influenced. The message is radical, but the cinema is an art. It is towards such a fusion that their work is directed.

Saeed Mirza graduated from the Film Institute in 1976, ten years after Shahani and Kaul. Eight years of working for an advertising agency had bred a fascination with films. He gave up one profession to prepare himself for the insecurity and adventure of another. After the regulatory three years at the Institute, he joined Mani Kaul, K. Hariharan and other graduates in the Yukt Film Cooperative*, whose first production was *Ghashiram Kotwal*. In 1978, the Cooperative produced *Arvind Desai Ki Ajeeb Dastan* (The Strange Fate of Arvind Desai), written and directed by Saeed Mirza. A young man's alienation from everything that surrounds him; his father's business which he sees as exploitative, his leftist friend and the heated discussions on Marxism, a visit to a brothel, the girl he goes out with, nothing seems to have any meaning. It is an intense young film. As Saeed Mirza said in an interview with Iqbal Masud,** looking back on *Arvind Desai* six years later, "It was very classic in construction... a film which could easily have been made by a person— like me— who had gone through an academic education about the theory of the construction and the structure of film and one who is well versed in existentialist philosophy and literature."

From the start, it was clear that Mirza was interested in the play of ideas, in the clash of individuals with their society, rather than with relationships. *Arvind Desai* breathes a young man's nihilistic despair. In *Albert Pinto Ko Gussa Kyon Ata hai* (What Makes Albert Pinto Angry?), 1980, the despair dissolves into an anger directed against the creeping cynicism, exploitation, class and communal arrogance and tensions in the city of Bombay. Pain and rage, bewilderment, the loss of innocence, a reluctant pragmatism, are all part of Albert Pinto's (Naseeruddin Shah) journey through a world whose rules he cannot grasp. A garage mechanic, he considers himself superior to his colleagues because the affluent owners of the cars he repairs treat him with easy friendship, until the wife of one of them tips him for bringing the car back, and he is forced into recognising his inferior position in the economic and social hierarchy. His Goan Catholic parents believe in the solid middle-class virtues of hard work and just rewards, but to Albert's irritation, his younger brother is a guitar-playing layabout. His lame sister (Smita Patil) smoulders with an inner anger. A bitter pragmatic, she understands the rules and the limitations of the games people play. When the father feels compelled to join a strike at the factory where he works, Albert is bewildered by what he sees as a betrayal of the principles on which he has been brought up, while his sister approves of and supports her father. His girl-friend Stella (Shabana Azmi) is a natural, unaffected extrovert. Albert is affronted by her

---

* *Film Miscellany,* Film and Television Institute of India, 1976 p. 4.
* See page 96.
** *Sunday Standard (Indian Express),* 15 April 1984.

Saeed Mirza's ALBERT PINTO KO GUSSA KYON ATA HAI, 1980

friendliness with his colleagues as much as by her boss' assumption that as a secretary — and a Goan at that — she should welcome his advances. The sub-text contains a biting, multi-layered commentary on the commercial cinema's arch conservatism and warped portrayals of woman. If she works she is invariably a young girl employed in a subservient position; if she does not wear a sari, she must be Westernized, therefore "modern and wicked"; if she is a Christian, she must be easily available.

For Albert, everything conspires to make him realise the wide class and caste differences of which he is a victim. Stella's brother dreams of emigrating to Canada, Albert's dignified, conscientious father gets beaten-up, his brother Dominic is arrested for a petty theft and lands in jail. Going to plead with Dominic's band of thieving associates, Albert is faced with the violence of those who flourish outside the pale of society.

The last scene of the workers procession, flaming torches lighting up the night, could have been a melodramatic underlining of the dividing line between oppressor and oppressed. Instead, the quiet understatement with which it is shot, invests it with a tragic dignity. Combining various genres and styles, Saeed Mirza uses narrative to stir sensibilities, offering discerning insights into the nature of the struggle of all minorities.

Albert Pinto is the personification of an idea. Mohan Joshi, the mild, elderly protagonist of Mirza's next film *Mohan Joshi Hazir Ho* (A Summons for Mohan Joshi), 1984, is that rare individual who feels a personal responsibility for the decay in the moral and ethical order, and resolves to do something about it.

In the four years that separate the two films, Bombay's downward slide as a city escalated rapidly. An exploding population which increases daily as people pour in from all over the country, dreaming of pots of gold or just a living wage; the terrifying tensions that result from overcrowding and the virtual collapse of civic amenities; the manipulations by unscrupulous "developers"; the corruption, the noise, the fear, the strife; Bombay, that most elegant of cities, has become the happy hunting-ground of an underworld which reaps enormous advantage from the chaos. Wealth, ill-gotten or legally acquired, is a potent social leveller. Today, in Bombay's small island of privilege, it is not unusual to have as one's neighbour a recognised smuggler.

For Mirza, evidently, the deterioration of life is too disturbing to be ignored, and his attitude towards his cinema has shifted accordingly. Through *Mohan Joshi* he wishes to communicate on a more immediate, urgent basis, than in either of his earlier films. Consequently, it is spelt out more clearly. The initial concern with cinema as art shifts firmly with *Mohan Joshi* into a political, activist cinema. Choosing the form of narrative, Mirza takes as his protagonist the unlikely figure of an elderly, retired minor bureaucrat. Mohan Joshi, sickened by the appalling conditions in the *chawl* (a block of tenements) which is the best he can afford in Bombay, is driven to taking the callous landlord to court for essential repairs and maintenance. He is supported by his gentle, courageous wife against the wishes of his son and daughter-in-law, who ask only to be left in peace to retain their fragile hold on middle-class respectability. A younger daughter innocently in love with a neighbour's son, sees the court action only as an obstacle to the prospective marriage they are romanticising about.

The major part of the film is taken up by the court case and all that it entails; the impoverishment of the old couple as the case drags on for years and the costs mount, the impassivity of the court, the physical threats to the family by the landlord's henchmen as well as legal cases manufactured against them by his unscrupulous lawyers, the other residents in the *chawl* whose derision of the old man turns into a grudging respect for his grit and determination, and finally to overwhelming support when they realise that his lonely fight might benefit all of them.

The world of the *chawl* is treated realistically, with the exception of the daughter and her boy friend whose attitudes and lovelorn behaviour are a parody of the commercial cinema's conventional romantic couple. The landlord and the lawyers are cleverly caricatured. The comic front of the landlord covers a menacing power. The two "promoters" who dog his footsteps, plan to demolish the *chawl* and replace it with a luxury high-rise apartment building. Their farcical appearance— black suits, dark glasses— is a satirical dig at the conventional villains familiar in the popular cinema.

Ketan Mehta's BHAVNI BHAVAI, 1980

The tragi-comedy, says Mirza, was designed to strengthen the basic idea of the film. Expediency and hypocrisy are the order of the day, but the conduct of individuals like Mohan Joshi and others within the system can stop the rot. In a reversal of the usual position, Mirza prefers the older couple as his protagonists because the generation that was young at the time of Independence has some dignity left, the young ones have become "frozen and static in their attitude to life."*

Saeed Mirza's films reflect his own evolution over eight years and three films. The question of cinema has become increasingly interlinked with history for him. Formalist concerns are being edged out by another commitment, a commitment to life itself. There is a quick impatience with all art forms in Mirza's reactions— "Where is the innovation in the cultural scene today?" he asks. "Where is it occurring? It is a reflection of the state we are in: static, regressive... in cinema we know what we are up against. Now is the time for intuition... not in a metaphysical sense but in terms of aesthetics. It is necessary to work on that. Because all criteria which we hold as sacrosanct have collapsed... look at the times we are living in. We are sitting on a volcano."

Mirza is not the only one who shows signs of a shift in perspective. Ketan Mehta's second film, *Holi* (The Festival of Fire), 1984, is in Hindi. The question of language is a significant pointer to a different approach. *Bhavni Bhavai,* (A Folk Tale), 1980, his first film, was in his mother tongue Gujarati— "I felt a need for direct contact with my people, to see things for myself." He made a Hindi version of it later, but by the time he started *Holi,* this concern had moved beyond regionalism into a wider national area and the language of the majority of the population.

Set in a small-town college campus and based on Mahesh Elkunchwar's Marathi play of the same name, *Holi* shows the eruption of violence among students. Unmotivated, spontaneous, it bursts out of the highly combustible conditions created by the intrigue and manipulations which go into retaining personal power, the injustices, callousness and indifference towards the students, the impotence of the rare individual who cares— in fact, the country in microcosm. The suicide of one of the boys at the end "is on a personal level but it is murder committed by society.. How can a society which ritually sacrifices the energies of its youth to sustain and perpetuate the contradictions of the system, be changed?" Mehta asks. For him, it is not a rhetorical question.

The question was raised in Mehta's first film as well but not posed with such obvious intensity. In *Bhavni Bhavai* he gave himself more room for play. It showed a delight in formal patterns. For *Holi,* he moved from a blend of folk form, realism, caricature, drama, farce and satire to another style altogether. The extremely long takes in *Holi* (40 shots in a film lasting 140 minutes) with the camera swooping, panning, circling, probing, acts as an alienating device in its own way, keeping you aware of what you are looking at, forcing you into reflection. It does not, unfortunately, always work in the way Mehta intends it to. Since the thrust of the film is dramatic, the repetition of certain scenes, particularly of the students in the canteen, becomes irksome even though the mood and the resolution in each instance is different. But the end is implicit in the beginning, and the film has few surprises.

The sync shooting gives the sound an immediacy and captures the tenseness of the moment, adding to the film an almost documentary flavour. There are some superb moments as, after the orgy of violence, comes a post-coitus melancholy. Grouped on the steps of their hostel, one voice after another takes up a song with no music to back up the strong, sombre young voices:

We are not used to life.

We have no time for death...

* Interview with Madan Gopal Singh in *Festival News* No. 7.

What kind of world are we going into now?

What journey is this, where does the path lead?

Almost as soon as *Holi* was finished, Mehta began shooting *Mirch Masala,* which he is now completing. He has begun to look on a film as an essay, with neither time nor inclination to develop its form fully. He seems haunted by the idea that time may be running out, for him and for the classical cinema as we have known it. In the nine years since leaving the Film Institute, he was able to make just two films. Perhaps that is the reason why he wants to rush into the third while he can. Graduating around the same time as Saeed Mirza, he went back to Gujarat (from where his family have moved to Delhi) and, inspired by the cooperatives set up by Adoor in Kerala, and Mani Kaul and others in Bombay, created the Sanchar Film Cooperative in Ahmedabad. The finances for *Bhavni Bhavai* came from the NFDC. For *Holi* he wanted full freedom and chose to finance it independently, putting into it everything he had earned through documentaries and television work.

Bhavni Bhavai was produced by the Cooperative. In it, Mehta makes brilliantly inventive use of the Gujarati folk form Bhavai, combining it in a startlingly original manner with a variety of other styles, to produce a film which is indubitably one of the high points in the short history of the alternate cinema.

It starts in a familiar enough fashion. The huts of the Harijans have been burnt down, and a group of small urchins ask an old man "why?" As an answer, the old man starts telling them a story popularly sung and performed in the Bhavai form of folk drama *Achhoot No Bhavai Vesh.* And the film shifts to the past, to the strange fate of Jivo, a dashing young Harijan who turns out to be a prince. The youngest queen of a foolish King (Naseeruddin Shah), jealous of the older queen's baby son, conspires to have him killed. The courtiers secretly put the baby in a box and set him adrift on the river. He is found by a harijan couple and grows up as their son. Ujaan, the gipsy girl he loves (Smita Patil) taunts him for wearing the degrading garb forced on the Harijans by the upper castes. She herself, free as a bird, defies him to discard it, and they run away together. But the wicked queen has discovered Jivo's true identity, and bribes a fortune-teller into warning the credulous King against danger from "a man called Jivo". He is caught and brought to the palace. At Ujaan's bidding, Jivo offers a bargain — his life for the Harijans' right to dress normally.

The surprise lies in the end. Two possible conclusions are both shown. One is a happy-ever-after ending; the other has the grimness of contemporary reality. The two are sharply contrasted as the film starts and ends in the present with the past sandwiched in-between. Naturalism and stylisation, a celebration of life, and despair at what people have made of it: Mehta uses the Bhavai form with its freedom to move between different styles in acting, speech, music, dance to reveal conditions instead of dramatising them. He draws upon a variety of other traditional Indian sources as well in an effective formal eclecticism that includes asides to the audience or depicting an event and going immediately into a social analysis of it. Brecht was clearly in his mind, and Mehta acknowledges the debt, adding, however, "Bertholt Brecht studied the epic structure from Noh and Kabuki theatre. If he had come to India he would have seen that Bhavai is also an epic form and freer in its capacity to make a point."* The debts are acknowledged but the result is uniquely personal, highly original. Gene Moskowitz wrote about *Bhavni Bhavai* in *Variety* (January 1981): "A delightful didactic fable with sharp Brechtian influences that work on practically all levels. This colourful film is inventive in its costuming (by Ketan's wife Archana Shah), playing, setting and imbued and digestible statements on authoritarianism and revolt."

* *The New Generation, 1960-1980,* ed. Uma da Cunha, Directorate of Film Festivals, New Delhi, 1981.

Brecht and Bresson, Fellini, Ozu and Bergman, Godard and Tarkovsky, Ghatak, Ray and Guru Dutt: that the initiation of the students at the Film Institute is extraordinarily vast is borne out by the styles they have developed in their own films. For Nirad Mohapatra, it is Ozu that he feels closest to, stylistically, temperamentally and culturally, saying, "Before I discovered Ozu, Bresson was my favourite. I like their quiet, meditative stance — maintaining an aesthetic distance. It shows respect for the audience and demands a qualitative participation. I like Bresson's form but it is difficult for me to react to his films and that, I think, is because of a cultural barrier. No matter how much I read of Christianity, about Jansenism, it never became a

Nirad Mohapatra's MAYA MRIGA, 1983

113

first hand experience for me. With Ozu it is different, much simpler because Hindus and Buddhists have a lot in common in their thinking, philosophy, attitude to life..."

Nirad Mohapatra graduated from the Film Institute in 1971 and went back to teach there for another two years. He drew on autobiographical elements for his film *Maya Mriga* (The Mirage), 1983, and waited eight years to make it in his own way. His brother Sampat, doubled as art director and actor (in the role of the successful second brother) in a cast of non-professionals. The NFDC provided the loan for which the Orissa Film Development Corporation stood guarantee.

The influence of Ozu shows in the meditative pace of the film, its detached observation of family life in a small town in Orissa, the undermining of traditional structures as new ways gnaw at its foundations. The style is restrained, understated; medium shots and slow, lingering pans match the elegiac temper of the subject, suggesting a nostalgic regret for a secure universe with the joint family as its centre, when relationships could be taken for granted and individuals fitted conveniently into given slots, no decisions were required, no special effort needed to be made. But bit by bit, Mohapatra bares the resentments, frustrations, stifled desires and suffocating closeness felt by those trapped in such a life, the deadening stagnation of a small town where nothing changes. The faceless unit — the extended family — is delicately picked apart to identify the individuals comprising it. No dramatic revelations, no deep psychological probing. Just the veriest hint that under the calm exterior lie strong emotions which, in all probability, will never be openly expressed. When the joint family does begin to split up, the collapse comes about in slow, measured degrees.

The traditional oppression of women is evident in the uncomplaining way the elder daughter-in-law carries out the routine tasks expected of her. Her husband takes upon his patient shoulders the traditional responsibility for the family, which devolves upon the eldest son. The second son successfully competes for the prestigious administrative service, and the family's pride in that achievement underscores the height of social aspiration. When his newly-wedded, city-bred wife refuses to stay on in the family home, and leaves with her husband, the seeds of disintegration are planted. The elder daughter-in-law is moved to a small gesture of protest. Her husband is stirred enough by it to a realisation that the price of his vacillation was paid by his wife's drudgery. He determines to take his own small family away to the city to build a separate life for themselves. The youngest of the four brothers is able to go to the college in Delhi he has been dreaming of when his successful brother (Sampat Mahapatra) agrees to support him. Reluctant at first, rationalising his reluctance, he is shamed into acquiescence when he realises that his salary is already higher than his school-teacher father's was at the end of his working life. Only the third brother is left with his ageing parents, all avenues closed. A poor academic record? Victim of a provincial sense of inferiority? The old grandmother watches over the disintegration in uncomprehending bewilderment. An era is ending.

Nirad Mohapatra could have used a more complex, richer form to portray the violence of change. But his formal concerns are clearly focussed on evoking and sustaining a mood through nuances and grey tones, rather than a rich characterisation which might upset the delicate balance. What interests him is the life within the confines of the rambling old house which is the film's setting. Saeed Mirza was moved by the film into a spontaneous tribute, ending a review-article with, "The clash between the past, present and future, parents and children, men and women, the traditional and the modern, all come under the film's ambit. How can one film encompass so much? *Maya Mriga* does and does it with the wisdom that is required when a subject so vast is being tackled."*

* To the author

* Saeed Mirza on *Maya Mriga* in *NFDC News,* February 1984, Bombay

Mohapatra plans to continue working in the same strain. His next film will be placed in a similar small-town milieu and will deal with working women, three school teachers waiting for something to happen in their lives — another calm exterior covering a burning undercurrent.

From meditative contemplation in a provincial town to wild comedy in the city, the alternate cinema provides an array of contrasts. But Kundan Shah's slapstick contains a very pointed sting. A 1976 graduate from the Institute, where he went after five years of trying out different professions, he knocked around for another three years. With a bunch of colleagues, they set up a cooperative of their own in Hyderabad on the assumption that there would be less competiton. Broke and unsuccessful even in their attempts to get assignments for documentaries and advertising films, Shah returned to Bombay. His break came when Saeed Mirza took him on as an assistant in direction and script for *Albert Pinto*. Assistant to Rabindra Dharmaraj on *Chakra* and then to Vinod Chopra on *Sazaaye Maut* (Death Penalty), and he was ready for his own *Jaane Bhi Do Yaaro* (Who Pays the Piper...), 1983. He won the script competition the NFDC had launched and the NFDC undertook the financing and production of the film.

In quick, inventive, cleverly contrived situations, the gags follow each other at a reckless pace. Saeed Mirza, for whose *Mohan Joshi* Shah was one of the group who worked on the script, says about him: "Kundan Shah is a vital force in scripting — *woh pagal hai* (he's wild) — he takes off in all directions — the original script of *Jaane Bhi Do Yaaro* has so many references but he brings them under control."*

Kundan Shah's JAANE BHI DO YAARO, 1983

* Saeed Mirza in an interview with Rajiv Rao and Rafique Baghdadi in *The Sunday Observer*.

K.N. Dhir's PRATISHODH, 1982,

Manmohan Mahapatra's NEERABA JHADA, 1984

Shah himself says it is only through entertainment and a narrative that audiences can be stirred into thought. Given the conditions in which film-makers and film-goers find themselves, the choices are reduced to a simple equation— simple structures plus audiences or complex forms plus critical acclaim. Shah opts for broad farce with a strongly critical social message. The two heroes of his film are well-intentioned innocents abroad who get taken for a ride by just about everyone. It is the fate of the honest, decent citizen today, Shah believes. Not only do the two bumbling, likeable heroes get cleverly exploited but they also get punished for their efforts. The film is full of surprises, and sequences that, even in retrospect, keep you laughing. But the message is never forgotten. Whether it is a dig at corruption, or at the dirty deeds in business or journalism, the common man or woman is a helpless pawn. Although the sudden, violent end is treated comically, it comes as a shock, subverting the genre and the expectations of the audience which anticipates a happy end. "The situation around us is bleak," insists Shah. "And it is necessary to make people feel that society itself must change. I made a comedy so people would come and see the film, and though comedies normally end with one more gag, I felt they should go away disturbed and think about what they had seen."

The witty dialogue is full of allusions to contemporary events immediately grasped by Indian audiences. It has some of the new cinema's favourites, Naseeruddin Shah and Om Puri playing uncharacteristic comedy with verve and the fine sense of timing necessary for comedy. Ravi Baswani, another National School of Drama graduate, was introduced by Sai Paranjpye in *Chashme Buddoor,* and shows himself a born comedian. *Jaane Bhi Do Yaaro* adds a welcome dimension to the scope of the alternate cinema.

Other individual films in different ways show traces of wanting to follow in the footsteps of Kumar Shahani or Mani Kaul or the Saeed Mirza of *Arvind Desai Ki Ajeeb Dastan.* But intentions do not necessarily spell success. The forms they adopt show the directors' cinematic education but fall short of capturing the hard inner essence which makes them significant. K.N. Dhir *(Pratishodh,* Retaliation), Vinod Chopra *(Sazaye Maut,* Death Penalty) Vishnu Ahuja *(Pehla Adhyay,* Chapter One), all graduates of the Film Institute, received loans from the NFDC to make their films. *Pehla Adhyay* reflects the isolation and increasing alienation of a young man, a college student, from his surroundings; *Sazaaye Maut* has a murder as its springboard; *Pratishodh* shows the utter helplessness of the victims of bureaucratic delays and corruption. Produced by the actress Kavita Nagpal, who also plays the main role along with K.K. Raina and Ram Gopal Bajaj of the National School of Drama, it has an intensity which, however, never changes its pitch. Dhir was a contemporary of Kaul and Shahani at the Institute, Mathur was an assistant on Kaul's *Ashad Ka Ek Din* and *Duvidha,* Shahani's *Maya Darpan* and Mrinal Sen's *Ek Adhuri Kahani.* Vinod Chopra made a much-applauded documentary, *Encounter with Faces.*

A contemporary at the Film Institute of Mohapatra, Mirza, Ketan Mehta, *et al,* Ashok Ahuja made *Aadharshila* (The Foundation Stone) in 1981. Like so many other film-makers who, by turns fascinated and despairing of their chosen field, are driven to making films about making films, Ahuja's *Aadharshila* too deals with the compulsive desire to make films. Obviously autobiographical, it is set in the Film Institute itself and has Naseeruddin Shah playing the Institute graduate who brings his newly acquired wife to show her the place where his fevered imaginings were born and nurtured. It is a tender, gentle film that burns with slow intensity. Asha Dutta, the only young woman to specialise in camerawork at the Institute, directed *Meri Kahani* (My Story) 1984 with the NFDC as producer-financier, almost immediately on leaving the Institute. With Goa as its unfamiliar setting, it has elements of Kundan Shah's comedy, but combines it with stark tragedy as gilded youth confronts reality. It lacks Shah's flair and, surprisingly, technical ability. Another recent graduate, Pankaj Parashar, was obviously influenced by Kundan Shah when he made *Ab Aayega Maza* (Now the

Fun Will Start) 1984. He uses many of Shah's techniques but the slapstick is too broad, the caricature too ridiculous for authentic comedy. But at least the idea of comedy as a genre is taking hold.

In Orissa, Manmohan Mahapatra, a distant relative of Nirad's and his student at the Institute, made the evocative *Seeta Rati* (The Winter Night) in 1982. A love affair in a small village fades out as quietly as the night is dispelled by the dawn, because the young man does not have the courage to stand up to his father, who opposes the marriage on the grounds of social and economic disparity. The young woman has the strength to face the future with resolution and no tears. In the next film *Neeraba Jhada* (The Silent Storm) 1984, he moves into a different rural environment where peasants have accepted their lot stoically for centuries. But today they have the courage to dream of a life of dignity. In their dreams lie the seeds of a more fulfilling future. The bleakness of the present is evoked through the silences and stark black-and-white photography which emphasises spaces and stillness. His next film *Klanta Aparanha* (Tired Afternoon), 1985, is in colour, but the colours are not the brilliant reds and yellows, greens and browns of the usual Indian countryside. They are the faded hues of old brick houses and peeling walls, of clothes that have been too frequently washed, carefully worn. Life continues, made up of small, transient joys and lasting struggles. In the strength of individuals, especially the women, Mahapatra sees the signs of survival and continuity.

In 1982 Jahnu Barua, one of the few Assamese to graduate from the Institute, made his first film *Aparoopa*. The beautiful green hills of Assam's tea gardens appear like a prison to the

Vishnu Mathur's PEHLA ADHYAY. 1982.

lovely, lonely young wife (Suhasini Mulay) for whom the reappearance of an old college boy-friend spells the possibility of escape — from isolation and from the understanding husband (Girish Karnad) who genuinely cares for her. The confrontation between the three is subtly and delicately etched. Financed by the NFDC, Barua made a Hindi version of this film and, while teaching cinema at St. Xavier's Institute of Communication in Bombay, is working on another.

Also from Assam, but not from the Film Institute, is Dr. Bhabendranath Saikia, a physicist and well-known writer who turned filmmaker in 1977. His latest film *Agnisnaan* (Ordeal), 1985, is revolutionary in its portrayal of woman. The caring, understanding, patient wife and mother, bows to her husband's decision to marry a second, younger wife and then, taking a lover, becomes pregnant herself. The husband whose physical advances she had spurned since he brought his second wife into their home, is stunned by her act. He is forced into silent acquiescence for to condemn her infidelity would be to admit his defeat. Visually lovely, its major shortcoming is its length (almost three hours), slow pace and an overstatement of its case.

M.A. Singh returned to Manipur from the Institute and with virtually no facilities, produced *Sanakeithel* (Golden Market) in 1984. Full of inevitable technical failings, its simple story with an undercurrent of hypocrisy and double-faced politics, it nevertheless has the stamp of sincerity. Earlier, in 1982, Aribam Shyam Sharma was the first to win international acclaim for Manipuri cinema when his *Imagi Ningthem* (My Son, my Precious) was awarded the top prize at the Nantes Film Festival. Its innocence and humanity exercise a universal appeal despite the lack of sophisticated technique.

There are fundamental changes taking place in society, even outside the metropolitan areas, and it is in the quiet statement of many of the films in the regional languages that one experiences them most deeply.

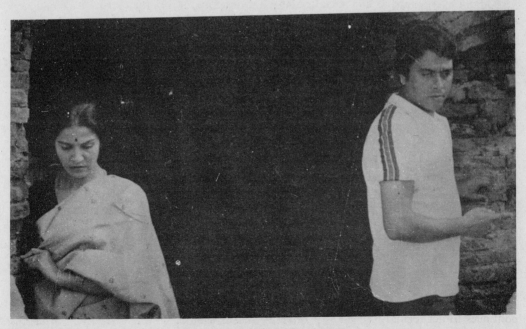

Jahnu Barua's APAROOPA, 1982

10

SUPPORTING CAST

The concepts of the new directors demanded a fundamentally new style of shooting, editing, acting, decor, sound and music. Technicians and actors used to the old ways would have been hard put to adjust to the sudden change required of them. Satyajit Ray's entire team for *Pather Panchali* was composed of new people with one exception, the art director, Bansi Chandragupta, and non-professional actors. Mani Kaul's crew and assistants were all Film Institute colleagues, as were those of all the Film Institute directors who started out subsequently. Shyam Benegal used the technical crew he had worked with on his documentaries and advertising shorts to shoot *Ankur,* but all the actors and actresses were playing their first roles.

Without like-minded technicians and actors, the directors, as they themselves say, could have achieved only a fraction of their aims.

The Players

The Pune Film Institute shaped the technicians and, for a short while in its early stages, the actors. The National School of Drama in Delhi took over when the Film Institute closed its acting course. With avenues of a profession in theatre severely limited, many of the NSD graduates turned hopeful eyes on the cinema. Naseeruddin Shah started the exodus. He went from the NSD to the two-year acting course at the Film Institute, and Om Puri was persuaded to follow suit. Initially very biased, as he says, against the kind of Hindi films which "didn't make sense after the NSD," Om Puri changed his mind when he saw that the cinema itself had started to change. "There was Hrishikesh Mukherjee, Gulzar and then I saw a festival of NFDC films......" It was no longer good looks but good acting that counted. He went to the Film Institute. His first real opportunity came in a small role in Karnad and Karanth's *Godhuli* in which Naseeruddin Shah played the lead. *Shodh* was his first main role. In eight years since then he has worked with the best of directors, including Satyajit Ray (*Sadgati*) down. The image of the hero in the popular cinema itself altered to accommodate the new notions. Om Puri, short, slim, the very antithesis of the tall, handsome hero, is now as sought-after in the commercial cinema as in the new. Naseeruddin Shah rose steadily to eminence from the start, although he too hardly conforms to the image of the conventional hero. Shah is more stubborn in his loyalty to the alternate cinema and to the theatre. With his wife Ratna Pathak, he continues to act regularly in plays— often at Shashi Kapoor's Prithvi Theatre— while his stature in films attains new heights with each role.

With Shah and Puri, the trickle from Delhi to Bombay began. It assumed the proportions of a flood with the film *Gandhi* which provided the NSD students their first film-roles. "It gave us some extra money and we took off for Bombay like Indian workers going to the Gulf countries," Neena Gupta, a rising young actress remembers. For Rohini Hattangady, her role as Kasturba Gandhi was the start of a distinguished film career. She also, with husband Jayadev the theatre director, continues to act on the stage, but shooting in both kinds of films leaves little time for the theatre. Anupam Kher, Kulbhushan Kharbanda, M.K. Raina, Manohar Singh, the list goes on......

Shabana Azmi went straight from the acting course at the Film Institute into *Ankur,* and on to the top as a fine dramatic actress. Initially, she revelled in all manner of roles in the popular cinema, from comedy to gun-toting avenger (in *Ashanti,* based on *Charlie's Angels*) as well as the films of, among others, Shyam Benegal, Saeed Mirza, Mrinal Sen and Satyajit Ray (*Shatranj Ke Khilari*). Her argument is that fame through stardom in the one helps sell the other to large audiences. Of late she has become very selective about what she is prepared to do in the commercial world. Both Shabana Azmi and Smita Patil are staunchly determined to shun roles "that show women in a negative light." Smita Patil, with no training in film or theatre, arrived at the top through experience. She was a newsreader on television when Shyam Benegal saw her and asked her to act in a film of his. Today she divides her time, and her status, between acting with Benegal, Shahani, Sen, Ray (*Sadgati*) and others, and as a star in the popular cinema. The main difference in the two lies, for her, in the way the roles are written— "In the new cinema you get roles where you have to perform. Here (in the popular cinema) you often do not have anything to do. It is usually a stereotyped role which anyone could do fairly easily." She adds that popular cinema has helped her to grow professionally. With no aids for creating the right mood, little help from the director or the co-stars, no props or moral support, the lines have to be said cold. And she says them, but brings to them a charismatic presence and a ring of conviction.

Sharmila Tagore, who appeared before the camera for the first time as Apu's wife in Ray's *Apur Sansar,* regrets her lack of training in acting. "I'm sure it helps if you know the technique," she says. "This way you get exhausted... I think knowledge makes you relax. You don't have to run two miles to create the effect that you have run two miles...."

Gopi is one of the most prominent theatre actors in Kerala with very clear ideas about acting, theatre and films. In a discussion with Mani Kaul in 1979, he talked about the sense of alienation an actor can feel in his own life, his approach to acting different roles in films.... "A character once performed must be entirely annihilated. All the mannerisms that developed and now appear associated with that character must be buried. This negation is the first step towards preparing a new role. It provides you with a new area of insecurity, both aesthetic and economic, becoming inventive, innovative. At any rate, if you can feel the film in its entire span, your own little performance is first seen as relative and thereafter destroyed. The circus manager in Aravindan's *Thampe* is a total stranger to Sankarankutty of Adoor's *Kodiyettam.*" Gopi played both these roles and, some years later, was one of the few *actors* to have appeared in a film of Mani Kaul's— *Satah se Uthata Admi.*

Deepti Naval, Mohan Agashe, Amol Palekar, Mamata Shanker, Srila Mazumdar and Farooque Shaikh all arrived on the scene with the new cinema. Playing a variety of roles, their commitment to the films and the directors comes from a basically similar sensibility. Most of them have some association with the theatre. Mohan Agashe is also a practising psychiatrist and a member of the Theatre Academy in Pune, many of whose plays have been directed by Jabbar Patel.

As the actors and actresses have started moving between the new and the popular cinema, some stars have decided that the former brings an aura of prestige which stardom does not offer. Raakhee acted in *27 Down* and is in Aparna Sen's new film *Paroma*. Rekha played in *Umrao Jaan* and followed with roles in *Vijeta* and *Utsav*. The most surprising entrant into the new cinema, in occasional roles, is Amjad Khan. As the villain in *Sholay* (the biggest, all time box office success, extremely well made by Ramesh Sippy who is known for his meticulous craftsmanship) he became a household word. Satyajit Ray got him to play the sensitive, poetic Nawab of Avadh in *Shatranj Ke Khilari*. Amjad Khan is back in Saeed Mirza's *Mohan Joshi*. Jaya Prada arrived from leading roles in popular Telugu and Tamil films to all-India stardom in Bombay's Hindi films. Her ambition, she said, is "to be a good actress, and to win a national award."

Attitudes are changing, inexorably, but slowly.

The Craft

K.K. Mahajan was a contemporary of Kaul and Shahani at the Film Institute. He achieved the historic feat of shooting Mrinal Sen's *Bhuvan Shome,* Basu Chatterjee's *Sara Akash* and Mani Kaul's *Uski Roti*— the three harbingers of the new wave. Since that time, he has worked on a wide variety of films. The difference, he says, is that "They (commercial films) aim for an ideal situation. When confronted with a difficult situation in a difficult location, we will not say we can't do it. We improvise, even if there are no lights, whereas they would ask for arc lights. They wouldn't suggest using a bed-sheet as an improvised reflector... The advantage of working with directors of small films is that you experiment. When the commercial filmmakers saw the results we obtained, they followed our example and moved out of the studios. But it was not easy for cameramen, who had worked for so long in the studios, to adapt." The strong, sharp lighting favoured by the commercial cinema is not, according to Mahajan, because they want greater depth of field but because "that is the kind of lighting they like". Naturally, much depends on the director. "There are some directors who conceive certain scenes with lighting effects in mind. Guru Dutt conceived the song in *Kaagaz Ke Phool* as a lighting effect, and the result (of cameraman V.K. Murthy's work) is good." For Mahajan too, the aesthetic quality of his work depends on the director. "Kumar Shahani is very particular about colour and texture, and conceives good camera movements. I have to enhance what he conceives. In Mrinal Sen's *Khandhar* there is a scene where a character walks down a corridor carrying a lantern. Mrinal Sen conceived that scene in terms of lighting... A scene like that in a commercial film would have the character and the background brightly lit... I use light to create patterns." *Pather Panchali* was the first film Subroto Mitra shot and, "with *Jalsaghar* and *Charulata* he matured into a brilliant cameraman. I think his understanding of light is unsurpassed," Mahajan says.

Virendra Saini is among the many camera students who saw *Pather Panchali* at the Film Institute. "I discovered cinema for the first time," Saini say. "Until then I had only seen the usual Bombay film and a few from Hollywood that played in the theatres." *Pather Panchali* was an experience from which it took a long time to recover. Saini has shot all of Saeed Mirza's films, some of Mani Kaul's, all of Sai Paranjpye's. He is not interested, he says, in the kind of job "anyone can do. It's impossible for me to work in the commercial film industry where the actor (or actress) arrives for an hour and the director has to rush to take the shot. No time is given to the cameraman to plan his lighting. All that is required is to register that star's face on the screen..." But adds Saini, "I am quite optimistic about the future because to some extent audiences have started noticing things like good photography." Audiences, and the film-makers themselves. Ramesh Sippy's latest film *Saagar,* a love story that took three years and a legendary sum to make because Sippy is a perfectionist, and could afford to reshoot as often as he wished, is visually breathtaking.

Ramachandra Babu, Madhu Ambat, Shaji, all graduated from the Institute and went on to transform the look of the cinema in Malayalam and Kannada. Balu Mahendra specialised in camera work and shoots all his own films. There are today a large number of these highly-trained cameramen working in both the new and the popular cinema, experimenting in the one, transfiguring the appearance of the other. With the rise of the new cinema came a new respect for craftsmanship, for sound and editing in addition to photography.

An awareness of the importance of art direction was born with, yet again, Satyajit Ray and his art director Bansi Chandragupta. He had worked on *The River* when Renoir arrived to shoot it in Calcutta in 1950. The authenticity of *Pather Panchali, Jalsaghar, Charulata...* owed a great deal to Chandragupta's sets. Finally, driven by economic necessity, he left Calcutta for Bombay, to be immediately adopted by the new young film enthusiasts. "The tycoons of Bombay's mass film industry would dub him expensive and finicky," Kumar Shahani wrote after Chandragupta's sudden death in 1981. "He would spray salt in the air... if a set were to represent a location by the sea." Nitish Roy, the young art director of Sen's *Khandhar* and *Kharij*, Nihalani's *Party*, Benegal's *Mandi* among others, never met Chandragupta but says he learnt everything from seeing his "flawless sets in so many films." "We have a grand tradition of elaborate, spectacular sets in India. But I think it is considerably more difficult to design the sets of a contemporary situation than it is, for instance, of a historical. It is really Bansida who brought a sophistication to Indian art direction." The main problem is the perennial one, lack of appropriate materials or technology. "We can't get the right colours, machines, materials. We can't use fibre glass, for instance, which was the basic material for Spielberg's *Close Encounters of the Third Kind* and is standard in set design everywhere in the world. Edging, moulding, all that one needs to provide that realistic finish is hard to come by, so one has to invent one's own. In *Party* we had designed a porch outside the main house and I wanted to use stained glass for it. We couldn't get any transparent paint here which is what was really required. My assistants had to hand-paint every single piece of glass for that effect. But even with these handicaps, skilled technicians are able to produce professional sets... There is much more sophistication than in the past. In the commercial film industry the situation is much better than it used to be."

From the enchanting sets Meera Lakhia created for *Bhavni Bhavai* to the deceptively simple authenticity of the house refurbished entirely by Sampat Mohapatra for (brother) Nirad's *Maya Mriga*, he art and the technique are growing slowly with the recognition of the importance of set design.

Music

Wherever one looks for the genesis of an idea, a technique, Satyajit Ray's name comes up with almost boring regularity. For *Pather Panchali*, Ray asked Ravi Shanker to do the music. Ravi Shanker, for whom it was a first essay, composed and recorded the music in one all-night session. He completed the trilogy for Ray and one other film that came in between, *Paresh Pather*. Two great contemporaries of Ravi Shanker— Vilayat Khan whose instrument is also the sitar, and Ali Akbar Khan the sarod maestro—did the music for *Jalsaghar* and *Devi* respectively. By then, Satyajit Ray was ready to compose his own music. Working with great musicians who were neither used to film nor to "being told what to do" had its own drawbacks, Ray says. "For example, in the *Music Room*, there was a scene which lasts three minutes and seven seconds. If I gave them this limit they said they couldn't play a piece of music which lasted three minutes and seven seconds. Ultimately, I made them play for four or five minutes and then edited it. It was very exacting editing work, but absolutely fascinating."

Aside from the technical difficulties, the idea of working with renowned classical musicians was novel and exciting. Ritwik Ghatak asked Ali Akbar Khan to do the music for *Ajantrik* two years after *Pather Panchali*. In Ray's films music enhances moods. Ghatak uses music to counterpoint them. Music sometimes replaces sound effects in *Ajantrik*. Years later Ray said, "My belief is that a film should be able to dispense with music. Half the time we use music because we are not confident that certain changes of mood will be understood by the audience, so we underline these with music... I have used very little music in my contemporary films and as much natural sound as possible."

Harmony or counterpoint, either way, a new thinking arose on music and the sound track itself. In a country where music and song are integral to any ceremony or festival, it would be difficult to dispense with it in films altogether. But the altered approach to cinema demanded a different aesthetic in all areas, including music. B.V. Karanth, Bhaskar Chandavarkar, Vijay Raghava Rao, and Vanraj Bhatia have both a thorough grounding in classical Indian music and a contemporary sensibility. Vanraj Bhatia is the exception who is equally familiar with Western classical music. They entered the world of film together with the beginning of the new cinema. Between them they are responsible for the music in the majority of the new movement's films.

Prospects

The conditions that gave rise to an alternate cinema were both financial and aesthetic. The constraints that limit its expansion and evolution are both economic and political.

Institutional financing has been available since the sixties, but distribution outlets are still a dream. It was a political decision to create institutions where the aesthetics, sociology, and history of film could be studied. Support was extended to the growing film-society movement, which helped considerably in spreading a new film culture and creating a taste for the nuances and subtleties of films that approximate more closely to art and realism than entertainment. It was through the actions of the government that notions of excellence in craftsmanship and acting were first planted, which grew steadily with the exposure to the best of contemporary world cinema at International Film Festivals. A major section at this Festival is the Panorama of Indian Cinema comprising twenty-one films chosen from out of the preceding year's production by a specially-constituted panel. The national awards presented annually by the President of India is a ceremonial occasion followed by a festival of national award-winning films. The award itself, a golden or a silver lotus, is accompanied by a cash prize the amount of which has grown steadily, and it is now a sizeable sum.

The formalist approach to film making, founded on a thorough knowledge of film theory, history and analysis, is a direct consequence of the training at the film institute at Pune- and the smaller, private but (State) government supported Adarsh Film Institute at Bangalore and the Adyar Film Institute at Madras. At Pune, the technical training is augmented by the regular screenings and immense library of films of the National Film Archive. Its branches at Bangalore and Calcutta are the first in what is planned as a country-wide network.

The political will that created conditions and a climate conducive to innovation and an imaginative approach to the actual making of films, has not been followed through into distribution and promotion. State governments fall in the same trap of offering subsidies, grants and awards, but backing away when it comes to exhibiting the finished work. Film societies have worked assiduously towards creating discerning audiences. In recent years, there has been a spurt in serious writing on the cinema with journals and daily newspapers giving plenty of space to film columns. This only serves to aggravate the complaint still common today— "How do we get to actually see these films?" For the film-maker, the problem is a much more acute one. Without commercial distribution, the films have no way of proving their financial viability or of building up public patronage that would relieve him/her from permanent dependence on government support.

The support itself is not without hazards. The loans given by the NFDC have to be refunded. As the interest accrues, filmmakers find themselves permanently in debt. As a matter of policy the award winning film is shown on the government-owned television national network the first Sunday of each month. This affords some relief, as a single screening can take care of the loan on a small-budget film; but it eliminates the faintest possibility of regular release. There are no *cinemas d'art et d'essais*. The big picture palaces have not converted into smaller units. Building regulations, rules governing the shape and size of cinemas have not kept pace with the time.

Extraneous events too, have a way of exercising their own tyranny. The sudden boom in videos and the rapid expansion of television is affecting the entire cinema scene. The patronage extended to the realist school is pushing out innovation. Many directors— Basu Chatterjee, Sai Paranjpye, Kundan Shah, Jabbar Patel, Shyam Benegal, Goutam Ghose, Sandeep Ray— are attracted by the captive audience and the financial gain represented by making popular serials for television.

As the serious Indian cinema is beginning to win international recognition and acquire maturity and confidence, its position at home remains precarious.

Index